Many people come;
looking, looking, taking picture.
Too many people.
No good . . .
Some people come, **see***.*
Good!
—Dawa Tenzing
Thyangboche Monastery
Nepal, 1973

Many people come, looking, looking

Galen Rowell

THE MOUNTAINEERS

The Mountaineers: Organized 1906
. . . to explore, study, preserve and enjoy the natural beauty of the Northwest.

Frontispiece
Sunrise behind the Trango Towers
Title page
Annapurna Massif from the Kali Gandaki gorge, Nepal

Copyright © 1980 by Galen Rowell. All rights reserved.
Published by The Mountaineers
719 Pike Street, Seattle, Washington 98101
Published simultaneously in Canada by
Douglas & McIntyre Ltd.
1615 Venables Street, Vancouver, BC V5L 2H1
Manufactured in Japan

Edited by Ed Reading
Designed by Dianne Hofbeck
All photographs by Galen Rowell

Library of Congress Cataloging in Publication Data

Rowell, Galen A.
   Many people come, looking, looking.
      Includes index
   1. Mountaineering—Himalaya Mountains.
2. Himalaya Mountains—Description. 3. Sports and
tourist trade—Himalaya Mountains. I. Title.
GV199.44.H55R68 1980   915.4   80-19394
ISBN 0-916890-86-4

Contents

Preface

This book describes three modern expeditions to three regions in the Himalaya. Interspersed through the three stories are chapters of history and commentary on the rise of mountain tourism in the three regions.

Several factors unite these accounts in a picture of the changing face of the Himalaya. The expeditions were all in the same year in the late seventies, each to an area recently opened to tourism, and all were successful. Each expedition was in a different country, so that the three major Himalayan nations are represented: India, Nepal, and Pakistan. With me on each expedition, among other members, was Kim Schmitz, a mountaineer I had known for a decade.

Each expedition was different.

Our ascent of Nun Kun in the Ladakh district of India marked a turning point in mountaineering. It was a commercial climb, arranged by a travel company; the ascent was made by paid guides and paying clients. This ascent of Nun Kun was the highest guided climb anywhere by Americans. It turned out to be the highest successful American-based expedition of the year.

The ascent of the 21,000-foot lower summit of Thorungtse in Nepal broke no records, but it showed what is possible for a small group of friends on a low budget. The accompanying 250-mile walk around Annapurna introduces a disturbing vision of the Himalayan future. Ease of passage has brought to these highest mountains on earth the same frenzied urban wildness that is making American national parks uncampable.

The book's culminating narrative describes our ascent of the Great Trango Tower in Pakistan, a fast-and-light climb in the renewed tradition of early exploratory mountaineering. The surrounding region, the Karakoram Himalaya, is wilder and far less populous than the mountains of Nepal and India, resulting in special problems and special joys for mountaineers and tourists alike.

The three regions into which these expeditions went had been open to visitors for less than three years, but the effects of tourism on the ancient lands and cultures were visible already and were accelerating.

This book cannot hold all the history of high-altitude tourism or account for all its effects. Nor is it unbiased. In many ways, it is a chronicle of my tastes as well as my joys, my fears, and the uncertainties that accompany every Himalayan mountain adventure.

The chapters of background information on Himalayan mountaineering, trekking, and tourism since 1950 will let our recent expeditions be seen from the views of the first explorers, the native residents, and visitors of all types.

These glimpses of Himalayan cultures and previous expeditions have been chosen not primarily for their historical importance, but rather for their colors and textures. Both the original mountain cultures and the people who come to visit them are part of a mechanism of change in a mountain region once thought to be unchangeable.

Ron Gervason Feb. 1983
Jackson, Wy.

Acknowledgments

Many people in many countries made this book possible. Starting just around the corner from where I lived in Albany, California, Mountain Travel U.S.A. gave me the opportunity to lead the Nun Kun expedition and the use of their superb Himalayan library. My inspiration for these three small expeditions in one year in place of a single big one came from conversations in Berkeley with the late Eric Shipton that underscored the philosophy expressed in his many books.

In Nepal, mother country of commercial trekking, I received boundless assistance in my research from Liz Hawley, Al and Jennifer Read, and Stan Armington. Data on visitation came from Mr. Dilli Raj Uprety and Mr. Y.R. Satyal of the Nepalese Ministry of Tourism. Peter von Mertens kindly loaned four priceless tapes of 1976 discussions recorded in the Khumbu with Sir Edmund Hillary, David Brower, and members of his trekking party. I wish to thank Hillary and Brower for their permission to quote from these tapes. Special gratitude goes to Pasang Sona, my sole companion on a later Khumbu trip, for showing me Sherpa life away from the bustle of expeditions and trekking groups. Also of great assistance were Jim Edwards, Charles McDougall, Ashish Chandola, Jimmy Roberts, and Dr. Peter Hackett.

The cornerstone of the story of mountain tourism came from Dr. Charles Houston, a member of the first group to visit the Khumbu, who not only gave hard facts, but also his innermost emotions. His critique of a draft of this manuscript added considerable accuracy and polish to the final copy.

In Pakistan, the Eustace and Newberg families of U.S.A.I.D. in Islamabad were helpful in immeasurable ways. The positive changes in tourism in Pakistan from my first visit in 1975 to 1977 were remarkable, and this fast evolution was part of my motivation for writing this book. Mr. Naseer Ullah Awan of the Pakistan Ministry of Tourism was especially helpful both in his home office and during a meeting in Kathmandu with Nepalese tourism officials.

In India I gained voluminous information from talks with Abdul Rashid Bakshi, Renee Chandola, Devinder Kumar, Mridulla Kumar, and Lakshmi Singh.

The input I received from the twenty-four members of the three 1977 expeditions was invaluable, although difficult to quantify. I owe debts that I am not able to note. Sometimes a person provided a whole new idea or tidbit of information; other times a clever turn of phrase I wrote in my journal came from a conversation now long forgotten. If I must single out one person, it would have to be Kim Schmitz, the only person to accompany me on more than one of the 1977 trips, and the best expedition partner I've ever had.

Before the first word was written, John Pollock of The Mountaineers Books encouraged the project. Ed Reading edited the manuscript and developed the book concept with rare insight. He is one of the few editors going who can "gently insist" on a change and pull it off with full respect for the author's intentions.

I dedicate this book to Jo Sanders, who shares my life and my love of the Himalaya, and has helped with the most difficult task of producing this book. She organized the Nun Kun and Around Annapurna trips, joined me on two Himalayan ventures, listened to endless revisions of the manuscript, and typed them. The title was also her inspiration, which she relayed to me from a pay phone in a Mill Valley Mexican restaurant.

Galen Rowell
Berkeley

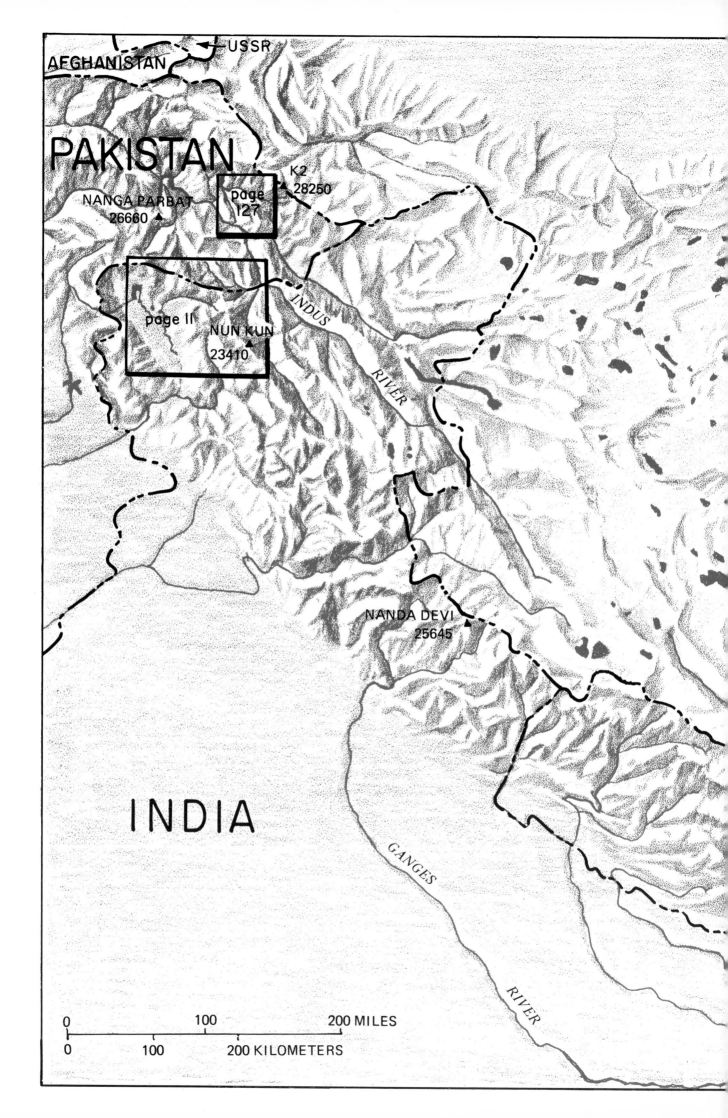

AFGHANISTAN

USSR

PAKISTAN

NANGA PARBAT
26660 ▲

page
127

K2
▲ 28250

INDUS

RIVER

page II

NUN KUN
▲
23410

NANDA DEVI
25645 ▲

INDIA

GANGES

RIVER

0   100   200 MILES

0   100   200 KILOMETERS

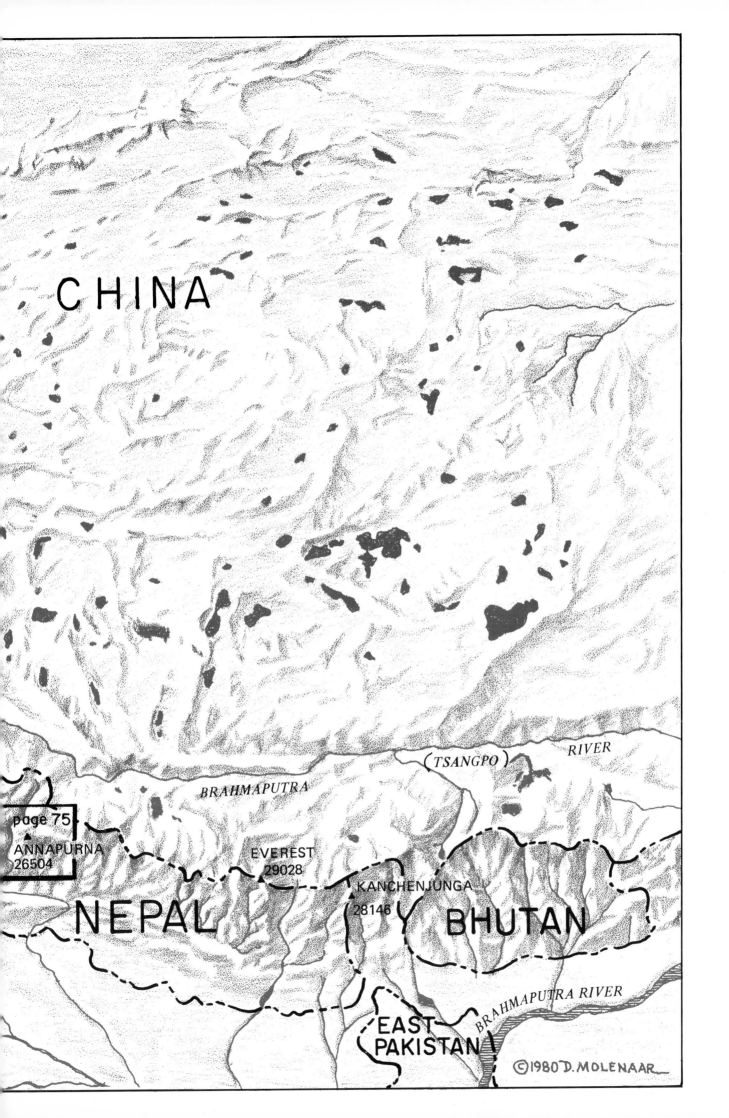

CHINA

(TSANGPO) RIVER

BRAHMAPUTRA

page 75
ANNAPURNA
26504

EVEREST
29028

KANCHENJUNGA
28146

NEPAL

BHUTAN

BRAHMAPUTRA RIVER

EAST-
PAKISTAN

©1980 D. MOLENAAR

1 | Mail-Order Mountaineers

Thirteen men boarded an Air India 747 bound from New York to Delhi. They appeared to have little in common. Some wore faded blue jeans; others sported coats and ties. A few wore double mountaineering boots onto the plane to beat weight limitations on baggage.

They were members of the first American expedition to Nun Kun, a 23,410-foot-high Himalayan mountain in the Ladakh district of northern India. They were traveling together because of a common desire to climb in the Himalaya. Their ages ranged from eighteen to fifty-seven, heights from five-foot-five to a foot taller. A few lived near the mountains in Colorado, California, and Oregon; others came from the lowlands of Illinois, South Carolina, Pennsylvania, and New Jersey. Among them were a professor, several doctors and lawyers, a salesman, a diplomat, a rural mail carrier, and a dishwasher.

The desire to climb a mountain was too thin a thread by itself to hold these men together. A stronger thread, hidden from view, had yet to be discovered and tested. Each of these men had made a commitment to join the expedition. A sacrifice of money, time, and personal risk had to be made in order to leave a world controlled by intellects and artifacts. Others, given the same choice, had remained home. Those who joined were not satisfied with brief glimpses of nature. Weekend trips into the mountains had only whetted their appetites for a long look at an untampered portion of the earth.

Now, ironically, the expedition traveled in a controlled environment: the cabin of an airplane. At thirty-five thousand feet, the temperature outside the cabin was forty below zero; inside, 375 persons sat in a subtropical climate

The Great Ice Plateau at 17,500 feet on Nun Kun

as the airplane moved along at six hundred miles an hour in stillness and quiet, without a breath of wind. James Hilton brought the word *Shangri-La* into the English language by a similar contrast between an airplane and the mystical appeal of the Himalaya. In his fictional vision, Shangri-La is a Himalayan paradise discovered by a pilot who makes a forced landing. Time stands still there, and people do not use their minds to alter natural beauty.

Much of the power of Hilton's vision is in the simple elements of fast travel to a timeless place with people yet unknown. These elements were present on the Boeing 747 bound for India. On the flight were Indian nationals in native dress, and the sights and smells of Asia had already begun. Babies cried. Stewardesses in saris spoke in several foreign languages. In this setting, the members of the expedition were getting to know each other; they had met for the first time in the departure lounge of Kennedy Airport in New York. I was the leader of this unusual group.

The expedition to Nun Kun was America's first commercial venture to a Himalayan summit over 7,000 meters. It was organized by an adventure-travel agency in California. An ad in a catalog sent to fifty thousand persons invited qualified climbers to respond. Twenty applicants out of the fifty thousand sent the required climbing résumé, references, and elaborate doctor's certificate. Thirteen were chosen.

My assistant leader was Kim Schmitz, a friend of many years. Between us, we had climbed previously with only one of the team, although we knew two others socially. The remaining names had no identity as living people. As we flew over the Atlantic, we pulled out the file of application forms and began to match information with faces.

Maynard Cohick showed the most vitality. He shook my hand with a strength that matched his features, and looked me in the eye. Maynard was a thirty-nine-year-old lawyer from Missouri whose weathered face was set on the energetic body of a teenager; he was small but robust. His outdoor experience was formidable, but not focused strongly on mountaineering. Before going to law school, he had taken several years off to sail around the world, working his way as a printer in port cities. He was a bicycle racer, long-distance runner, and skier. A year earlier, he had climbed Mount McKinley with a guided group, and now he wanted to try something higher. The last sentence of his application said, "I enjoy the strain of hard tasks and always do more than my share." As I watched Maynard walk down the aisle with a bounce in his step, I hoped he would still have that eagerness at 23,000 feet, where economy of motion and persistence go better than brute strength. I had a feeling that Maynard was going to be on the first summit team.

Tim Treacy was another lawyer, six years older than Maynard Cohick, and without Maynard's display of great energy. Tim was tall and slender and wore large spectacles that accentuated his narrow cheeks. He was quiet, and I remembered seeing him at a party where he had worn a bow tie; he had looked like the meek hotel owner in a cheap Western who emerges from the closet after his place is broken up by desperadoes.

It came as a surprise that Tim was a fine marathon runner, who regularly broke three hours for the twenty-six-plus miles. He had made many first ascents in the High Sierra, and had been on major mountains of every continent: Aconcagua and Chimborazo in South America, Kilimanjaro in Africa, McKinley and St. Elias in Alaska. Just six months earlier he had been on

Dunagiri (a 23,000-foot peak in India) with a private expedition. The climb was abandoned after four of his friends were killed in two falls. He felt a need to try a Himalayan mountain again before he lost his touch.

Sitting near Tim was Tom Smyth, another quiet man in his forties, a professor from Pennsylvania. Much of his experience, which spanned nearly thirty years, was as a leader for college outings on easy peaks and local rock climbs. I was surprised to see that he had listed "Fossil collector in Wyoming, summers 1948-49," among his qualifications for climbing in the Himalaya. When I asked him about it, he said that those fossil trips had produced internationally important discoveries and had resulted in meetings in the Tetons with Fritz Wiessner and Robert Underhill, two pioneers of technical climbing. He traced a lifelong interest in climbing to those summers in the mountains.

Almost incidentally, Tom asked if I read Loren Eiseley's nature writings. Eiseley was already well known as a paleontologist in the late forties, and he came to Wyoming one summer after learning the significance of the fossil site where Tom was working. Tom's strongest memory of Eiseley was that he made solitary visits to the bars of Casper, Wyoming, where he played pinball machines with great concentration long into the night, like a character out of one of his later works.

Malcolm Jones, a twenty-eight-year-old stock broker, was one of the youngest team members. He had begun outdoor activities with the Dartmouth Outing Club. Since graduating from college he had spent a week or two each year climbing mountains, usually with a climbing school. Although he possessed far less experience than the other members, he came with a solid recommendation from another Mountain Travel leader. On meeting him, I was glad to see a strong and energetic man behind weak credentials.

Gordon Benner was the largest of the clients, and also the most experienced. He stood six-foot-five, weighed 200 pounds, and had the biggest hands I have ever seen on a human. I had known Gus, as he preferred to be called, for more than a decade both through local meetings of the American Alpine Club and as my physician. He was qualified to be the expedition's leader. His climbing experience included not only technical routes in Yosemite and the High Sierra, but also new routes up Mount McKinley and Mount St. Elias in Alaska. This hard climbing, combined with experience leading a trek in Nepal, great physical strength, and gentle ways of dealing with people, made Gus an ideal member of an expedition. We had never climbed together, but I felt a strong bond of friendship, as if we had already shared good times in high places.

Rich Nowack was a big, mild-mannered man from Southern California. He worked as a dishwasher in order to pay for one mountaineering trip a year. He had made one trek in Nepal and several climbs in Mexico, Ecuador, Peru, and Algeria. His desire was not so much to stand on Nun's summit as simply to participate in a Himalayan expedition. Rich's attitude would help offset the competitiveness lurking within every expedition that has more members than summit berths. The combination of calmness and energy that he exhibited was contagious.

Larry Gibbs, thirty-five, was a sales manager for a machine equipment firm. He had climbed Mount McKinley and many of the important mountains of the West.

Arthur Mudge, forty-seven, was director of the U.S.A.I.D. mission in Nicaragua. He had climbed high peaks in Bolivia and Peru.

Pat O'Donnell, thirty-eight, was vice president of a Colorado ski resort. He had climbed extensively in Yosemite as well as on Mexican volcanoes and on Mount McKinley.

Bernie Najaka, thirty, was a New Jersey lawyer now living in South Carolina. He had made several ascents in the Alps and had done snow and ice climbing in the eastern United States.

Peter Cummings, thirty-two, a physician, had climbed Mount McKinley, two peaks in Peru, and dozens of snowy mountains in the Northwest.

Norman Benton, fifty-four, a rural mail carrier from Oregon, had the most high-altitude experience of all of us. His application listed eighteen ascents over 17,000 feet and two trips to the Himalaya before the form ran out of space.

The one member of the expedition not on the airplane with us was Chris LaRocca, an eighteen-year-old Dartmouth student who had stayed behind to finish his final examinations. He would join us in the Himalaya, at Srinigar. By far the youngest member of the expedition, but unusually mature for his age, Chris had done snow and ice climbing in the United States and in Peru.

Kim Schmitz's qualifications for climbing in the Himalaya were not as strong on paper as those of some of our clients. His résumé did not reflect the hot desire to reach the highest points of nations and continents that I saw in the repeated mention of McKinley, Aconcagua, Whitney, Mont Blanc, and Kilimanjaro on many other applications. Kim had never been over 20,000 feet before, but he had worked for many years as a mountain guide. He had been to the Himalaya three times as a trek leader.

Kim looked like the archetypal mountaineer. His facial features were almost a caricature of Nordic strength, set off by a deep tan and pale blue eyes as big and wide as those in a Keene painting. His upper body was strikingly broad, yet his hips and legs were as slender as a distance runner's. A writer once described him as a cross between Captain Marvel and Conan the Barbarian.

If Kim had spoken with a growl, it would have seemed in keeping with his appearance. All who met him for the first time were surprised that his voice was soft and he wasted no words. His way of life matched his manner. He had a knack for developing tremendous abilities without involving himself in either competition or public acclaim. During the sixties he had been a top Yosemite rock climber, making first ascents and climbing big walls in phenomenally fast times with his best friend, Jim Madsen. Together they had planned to become experts in high-altitude mountaineering, but not long after their first expedition to South America, Madsen fell the entire way down the face of El Capitan during an attempt to rescue stormbound friends. Kim drifted away from the Yosemite scene at the time that outsiders began taking it seriously. He lived in Squaw Valley and became an unusually talented skier but steered clear of competitions.

By 1977 Kim was ready to try something new. Several of his friends were past or present world record holders in speed skiing, and they invited him to enter the next trials. He had always held his own free-skiing with this fast crowd, and they thought he had a good chance of placing in the world's top ten the first time out. He had planned to go with them to the trials, until he and I met by chance and talked about climbing the Himalaya.

Right
Under the
west face
of Nun
Lower right
The 1977
American Nun Kun
Expedition

I had known Kim from Yosemite in the sixties, but we had never done any serious climbing together. We discovered that we had been on the same Sierra Club pack trip when I was thirteen and he was seven (although we couldn't remember each other). Kim told me that he longed to do alpine climbing in the Himalaya with small expeditions. He would be a fine assistant leader for Nun Kun and an ideal teammate for a private expedition to the unclimbed Great Trango Tower in Pakistan later that season. He dropped his speed trial plans to join both expeditions.

Our 747 stopped to take on passengers in London, Paris, and Frankfurt. As we headed across the Middle East toward Tehran and eventually Delhi, every seat was full. Kim and I sat together, and a French woman across the aisle followed our movements as we talked to various people wearing mountain boots. She asked where we were going, and I told her that we were an expedition bound for the Himalaya. "Another expedition in this plane is also going to the Himalaya," she replied.

"You must have talked to some of our members; they are not all sitting together."

"No. This is another expedition. Where are you going? To what mountain?"

"Nun Kun in Ladakh."

"That is where they are going."

"It must be our group."

"No. They are from France. Just a minute, I will return."

To our great surprise, the woman came back with a stocky passenger in tow. "Meet Mr. Sylvain Saudan," she said, "the leader of an expedition to Nun Kun."

Saudan was a short man of forty with thighs the size of beer kegs. He was legendary for ski descents of steep mountains. In Europe he had skied the west face of the Eiger and the Grandes Jorasses, and in America he had skied Mount McKinley. Now he sought to ski from the top of Nun Kun; his would be the highest ski descent in history from the summit of a mountain. (Miura, "The Man Who Skied Down Everest," had never climbed to the summit; he had begun his straight schuss from 3,000 feet below the top.) Saudan planned to make linked turns down a fifty-degree face that had never been climbed.

Saudan gave us disturbing information about Nun Kun. Kim and I had been led to believe that it was an easy climb. Now Saudan told us that his expedition to the mountain the previous fall had failed to reach the summit because of steep ice and bad weather. A Czech expedition earlier that season had succeeded in making the fourth ascent by a new route up the northwest ridge, but they had used five thousand feet of fixed rope on the upper sections. Kim and I looked at each other, realizing that we were responsible for the well-being of clients on a mountain that had turned back a man of Saudan's competence.

We were surprised that the government had allowed two expeditions on the same mountain at once—it is rarely done. Our mountaineering visas were held up somewhere in the Indian government; the Home Ministry had cabled us that visas would be granted when we arrived. I wondered what I would do if permission to climb the mountain were refused after we entered the country.

Just before going to sleep for the final hours of the flight, I wrote in my diary, "My fear on this trip is that we are so reliant on the performance of people whom we do not yet know." As leader, I was head of a logistic organization that was complex enough to boggle a corporate attorney. I was working for an American travel company, but a totally separate Indian company was bound by contract to supply transportation, porters, and food for the expedition. They, in turn, had subcontracted much of that task to Colonel Narinder Kumar, climbing leader of the successful Indian Everest Expedition and something of an entrepreneur. But Colonel Kumar had taken on leadership of an expedition to Kanchenjunga, so he had given over the task of supplying our Nun Kun expedition to his wife, Mridula, and his brother, Major Devinder Kumar.

Most of our basic necessities for climbing the mountain were to be waiting for us in India. It felt odd to be leader of an expedition without having checked off every piece of equipment before leaving America. I had a list of what was to be in India, but I wanted to see it with my own eyes. And it was not so much tents, stoves, and climbing gear I was worried about as the promised "five Sherpas from Darjeeling who have previously been on the mountain and know the area."

In Ladakh, no tradition of climbing and trekking had been established. The Ladakhis, unlike the Sherpas of Nepal, had no experience on high mountains. Nun had been climbed only four times before, and two of those climbs had been since the area was opened to tourism in mid-1974. It had been closed for twenty years. None of the higher peaks had been attempted by a modern American expedition, and I guessed that the keys to our success were as likely to be found in low-altitude organization and permissions as in technical problems up high.

2 | The Lama of Nun Kun

The tiny mountain kingdom of Ladakh was still locked in the Middle Ages in 1953. Most of the populace lived in stone huts, where light came only from the sun or an open flame. There were no motor vehicles, no gasoline, and no electric power. Even such basics as the chimney and the wheel were rarely seen. Chimneys were wasteful of heat in this cold land where wood was sparse. The wheel was less useful than the foot on the rock-strewn slopes of the Trans-Himalaya.

Ladakh seemed the same as in the days of Ghengis Khan, yet something was missing. The villages were quiet, more quiet than they had been in fifteen hundred years. They had the look of ghost towns.

What was gone was a network of trade with neighboring provinces that had once stretched for a thousand miles across Central Asia. The paths of Mongol armies had become trade routes, linking Tibet, India, and Central Asia. Caravans bent to the earth with silk, musk, wool, and gold crossed the Himalaya before Ladakh rose from the realm of legend into history. The trade went to Leh, the capital of Ladakh, where a few thousand souls lived by their wits in a land too high and too dry to be supported by agriculture alone.

In 1947, forces beyond the Himalaya called a halt to the timeless travel of the traders. Sir Cyril Radcliffe, a British judge, had come on a special mission: the partition of India. Drawing a line on a map, he divided India, the home of 350 million people, into two nations: an independent India and the new country of Pakistan. By so doing, he affected more Asian lives than any Westerner in history. The British tried to create a border that was fair, but it was not possible to be fair to everyone. Radcliffe's line separated orchard from

The upper part of Nun; original route on foreground ridge and 1977 route just below left skyline.

marketplace, child from parent, factory from employee. It stopped before it reached the Himalaya.

Like a crack in a pane of glass, Radcliffe's line remained its original length only while all was still. In Kashmir, a vote was to decide whether the Himalayan kingdoms that make up that region would become part of Pakistan or part of India. Instead, open war between the two nations split the subcontinent in half, continuing Radcliffe's line northward until it bisected Ladakh. When the fighting subsided, the extension of Radcliffe's line was called the cease-fire line. Not even locals were allowed to cross it. Ladakh's capital city of Leh became part of Indian Kashmir, sealed off from its commerce with Pakistan to the west.

In 1949, the Chinese closed Ladakh's northern border into Sinkiang province; a year later they closed the eastern border into Tibet as well. Leh was connected to the outside world only by foot. The route was south through the Vale of Kashmir. For eight months of the year, even this route was closed by deep snow on the mountain passes, leaving Ladakh in isolation.

The great rain shadow of the Himalaya left Leh high and dry. Even the South Asian monsoon was wrung dry when it arrived, after leaving its moisture as snow on the mountains. Skies as crystalline as autumn's came in every season of the year, and Leh received less moisture than parts of the Sahara Desert. The land was treeless except where loving hands had planted them, following Buddha's belief that a single tree was a nobler object than a prince in his coronation robes.

On the outskirts of Leh were the camps of Tibetan refugees and nomads from the plains of Changthang, who were among the few people able to continue their trade unhampered by politics. They raised Pashmina goats that needed pasturage above thirteen thousand feet. The goats produced wool of legendary quality that was shipped to the Vale of Kashmir, where it was woven and sold to the wealthy few who could afford it. Just beyond the town, seemingly at arm's length, a crescent of snowy domes glistened against the tawny moonscape like a necklace of pearls against bare flesh.

Ladakh was called Little Tibet, and Leh looked like a Tibetan city. Monasteries reminiscent of Lhasa dominated rows of houses, portals, and open shops. Beyond the center of town, the Shey Gompa held a giant Buddha that fixed a steady gaze over the heads of mortals. Nearby was the recently abandoned royal palace, home for a long line of monarchs who traced their roots to Tibet.

Buddhist men wore their hair shaved in front with long curls in back, a custom emanating from a ninth-century Tibetan king. Wiry and taller than most Asians, the men wore high hats and heavy woolen robes girdled at the waist. Women looked like royalty in decorated robes and dark, cobra-shaped hats topped with turquoise the color of a glacial lake.

There were Muslims, too, but except for a small mosque their presence was almost unnoticeable. Muslim men usually wore the same long robes as the Buddhists; their women, following Islamic custom, were seen as little as possible. Religious conflict was rare. Buddhist shrines were open to everyone and intermarriage was allowed. There were no taboos of food or dress. During festivals, which were frequent, dancing was for all to enjoy. Whole fields of barley, nurtured through the arctic climate, were converted into *chang*, a beer that helped keep life from getting too serious.

The year's largest festival was held at Hemis Gompa, a monastery

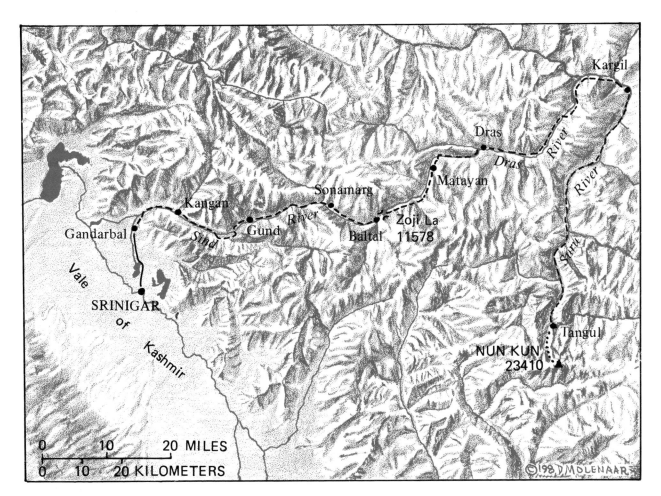

Nun Kun route

twenty-five miles from Leh. In June, 1953, even though the borders were closed, thousands of Ladakhis made the pilgrimage to the ten-day celebration of the birth of Padma Sambhava, the founder of Tibetan Lamaism. The Lamas governed nearly all aspects of society from art and medicine to cultivation and education, and every family had at least one relative among the fifteen hundred Lamas in Ladakh. The Lamas joined the festival.

At the festival in 1953 was a man with fair hair clipped short in back without the characteristic Ladakhi curls. Like the other men, he wore a long woolen robe and spoke Tibetan. Taller than the rest, he had blue eyes that peered at the world through round glasses with steel frames. His name was Pierre Vittoz.

Vittoz was a Protestant missionary from Switzerland. He had spent three years in Leh, and he seemed an intimate part of the Buddhist culture. During his tenure he had converted more natives into chess players than into Christians. He had made the best of a situation in a land where religion was already strong. His efforts were focused toward education, a small newspaper, medical care, and the writing of a Tibetan-to-English dictionary.

During the temperate summers, Vittoz had often slipped away into the mountains and scrambled up snowy summits; he had made several first ascents of peaks over 20,000 feet. Just the previous fall he had explored a mountain sixty miles to the south that was the highest summit along a 450-mile section of the Himalayan crest. Known to the local Buddhists as Shel Changma, "the Crystal Willow," it rose 23,410 feet into a white cone, far above anything in sight except for a twin summit, part of the same massif, two hundred feet lower and several miles away. The Kashmiri Muslims called the two Nun Kun. Nun was Shel Changma, the Crystal Willow. Kun, the lower peak, had an easy slope that an Italian count had climbed with a guide in 1914. Nun had been attempted by several expeditions but remained unclimbed.

Vittoz was captivated by the idea of climbing Nun, but he realized he couldn't do it alone. He reconnoitered the west ridge and made plans for a return visit with competent climbers. Afterwards, he wrote of his interest in the peak to a close friend in Switzerland, Marcel Kurz, an older mountaineer who edited the prestigious annual book series, *The Mountain World*. Kurz gave Vittoz's name to a French expedition that was planning to attempt Nun the following summer, and Vittoz was invited to join. The expedition was to be led by Bernard Pierre. Vittoz then discovered that the Indian government wouldn't let him leave Ladakh. Like Shangri-La, Leh was apparently easier to enter than to leave.

Walking through the festival at Hemis, Vittoz thought of the Crystal Willow; he contemplated its whiteness, the purity of its form, and his desire for it. He had had a chance meeting with the Indian Minister of Defense, who had traveled through Leh. He wondered if the minister would keep his word about taking Vittoz's problem all the way to Prime Minister Nehru if necessary.

A few days later, after the festival, Vittoz received a wire from Delhi. Not only did he have authorization to leave Ladakh, but he would fly out on a military plane, a privilege normally not given to civilians. With his heart pounding, Vittoz packed the clothes and equipment he would need for the months to come. They fit into a rucksack and a flight bag. Before leaving, he lettered a sign for the door of his mission: "The pastor has gone to the presence of the Most High!"

On July 14, Vittoz joined the French expedition in the hot lowlands of Kashmir. Although Nun was actually in Ladakh, he had to travel hundreds of miles out of the way to the south, since the direct approach route came too close to the Pakistani cease-fire line, and the expedition wasn't allowed to follow it. Although still in the Himalaya, he found himself in a world totally different from his own Ladakhi high country. The caravan passed through jungles filled with monkeys, snakes, and mosquitoes, and it lived mostly off the land. During the next two weeks of travel, he watched his world reappear with each bit of elevation gained. The expedition established base camp at 15,500 feet on July 29.

The expedition included a woman, Claude Kogan. The year before, Kogan had set the altitude record for an all-woman climb on 19,685-foot Quitaraju in Peru. On that expedition she also had made the first ascent of Salcantay with Bernard Pierre and four Americans. Pierre was continuing the concept of multinational expeditions by including four Frenchmen, two Indians, one Swiss, and six Sherpas on the Nun Kun team.

The most seasoned high-altitude climber of the expedition was not a European. Ang Tharkay, the sirdar, or leader, of the expedition's porters and coolies, was barely five feet tall, knock-kneed, and illiterate. A shy little man—but bursting with energy and wit—Ang Tharkay had spent far more time over 20,000 feet than his more famous companions, Eric Shipton and Edmund Hillary.

Had Ang Tharkay been able to write, his résumé could have been taken for an outline of Himalayan climbing history. During World War II he had worked for the Great Trigonometric Survey of India, trekking through the mountains of India, Sikkim, Nepal, and Kashmir. He had established the high camp for Herzog and Lachenal on the first successful climb of an 8,000-meter peak, Annapurna, in 1950. He had gone to Kanchenjunga with the Germans in 1931 and to Everest with the British in 1933, where he reached the high camp at 27,400 feet without oxygen. He had been Eric Shipton's righthand man on eight expeditions, including Nanda Devi in 1934; Everest in 1935, 1936, and 1938; Karakoram explorations in 1937 and 1939; Everest in 1951; Cho Oyu in 1952. On most of these climbs he had served as sirdar and occasionally as rope leader. Shipton called him "the best Sherpa I have ever known."

He had seemed destined also to be sirdar for the first ascent of Everest, but it did not happen. Shipton had been chosen to lead the 1953 British expedition, but he was then summarily replaced—a move that bitterly divided the community of climbers—with Colonel John Hunt, a military tactician. Tenzing Norgay was chosen as sirdar. Shipton's favorite Sherpa, Ang Tharkay, was not included in the crew.

Shipton's downfall came from his insistence on lightweight tactics. Hillary, who had climbed with Shipton for the past two seasons, also favored a small expedition and he very nearly withdrew from the team. Ang Tharkay was invited to Dhaulagiri with the Swiss and, later in the year, to Nun Kun with the French. Were it not for Shipton's misfortune, surely the most experienced high-altitude mountaineer of his generation would not have been assisting a group of relative unknowns on Nun Kun.

He expected to climb Nun Kun with city Frenchmen, and he thought he knew what to expect. He was not at all prepared for Pierre Vittoz, who spoke to him in Tibetan. Their dialects were different, Sherpa and Ladakhi, but the two

THE FOREST IS A PECULIAR ORGANISM OF UNLIMITED KINDNESS AND BENEVOLENCE THAT MAKES NO DEMANDS FOR ITS SUSTENANCE AND EXTENDS GENEROUSLY THE PRODUCTS OF ITS LIFE ACTIVITY. IT AFFORDS PROTECTION TO ALL BEINGS. OFFERING SHADE EVEN TO THE AXEMAN WHO DESTROYS IT. "GAUTAMA BUDHA"

men made an instant connection with each other. A devout Buddhist, Ang Tharkay led the other Sherpas in Buddhist rituals. When he learned that Vittoz was a man of the cloth, he referred to him as "the lama." Vittoz asked him how such a religious man could possibly practice Buddhism on a big mountain. Ang Tharkay replied, "On expeditions we live like chickens; we do not try to reach heaven."

During the first weeks, the expedition was besieged by snowstorms. Ang Tharkay prayed repeatedly for the sky to clear. Once, a snowstorm actually gave way to sunlight moments after his incantation, but on the next day the snow returned with renewed vigor.

The situation was becoming grave. July had been unusually dry; August was bringing unprecedented new snow. Some coastal towns were recording double the rainfall of any August in history. A hundred miles to the northwest, the American K2 team was pinned down in a ten-day storm at 25,000 feet.

Despite the weather, the expedition established its camps on the mountain. Camp I was placed at 17,700 feet on the edge of a great plateau of ice that stretched for miles below the final 6,000-foot thrust. Camp II was at 19,200 in an icefall just beyond a formidable rock tower. Camp III was at 21,000 feet, still in the icefall and below some towering ice seracs.

The morning of August 22 dawned gray, with six people imprisoned in the high camp. Bernard Pierre, Michel Desorbay, Pierre Vittoz, and Claude Kogan were the summit team. Jean Guillemin (the doctor) and Ang Tharkay were in support. Monsoon clouds had rolled in and consumed the mountain in a whiteout. Two Sherpas who tried to bring provisions from Camp II were unable to follow the marked route. After wandering from serac to serac, they retreated. That night the wind blew as never before and all but buried the tents in fresh snow. The climbers made a unanimous decision to go down, but they could barely see an arm's length ahead through the heavy mist and falling snow. Nothing remained of the old track. None of the wands with yellow flags were visible, even though the route had been marked only two days before.

Leaving tents, shovels, fuel, and cameras behind, the six climbers stumbled out into the storm. After a hundred yards of uncertain travel, Vittoz gave the lead to Ang Tharkay, who set off absolutely blind into a constant whiteness where earth met sky without a boundary. No one thing guided him. He used his unusual memory for tiny details of the terrain, his innate sense of location, and also a sixth sense that he couldn't explain. One by one he came upon the tiny yellow flags in the snow, and he remembered where the route doubled back steeply upon itself. The soft snow worried him as he inched across the forty-degree flank of a dome.

The rhythmical crunching of footsteps was broken by a slight noise, as if someone had quickly zipped up a parka. Then came a louder noise, building into a crescendo like the sound of rapids near a great drop. The entire slope was moving, and with it all six climbers. Guillemin and Vittoz were able to make ice-axe arrests in the hard snow below the sliding mass. Roped to these two, Kogan also stopped falling. The other three became part of the seething entity that continued to slide down the mountain.

Ang Tharkay tumbled like a rag doll. Nothing he did seemed to change the course of his fall. Blocks of snow knocked the wind out of him, and the rope pulled at his chest with frightening force. He did not question his own life or death; he waited for the situation to present him with an opening, however

Overleaf
*Moonlight on the
Great Ice Plateau
at 17,500 feet
on Nun Kun massif.*

brief or small. He felt his speed slow down, and he seemed to be floating weightlessly in space. Then the rope came taut and a mysterious force tried to pull him along even faster than the rate of fall.

Suddenly everything was still. Blood poured from his mouth, and his chest felt as if someone were standing on it. His eyes caught two forms in the snow. One was a whole person lying on the surface; the other was a separate human hand.

Ang Tharkay dove for the hand and began digging furiously. He came to a head that was very still. He himself could barely breathe and the pain in his chest was acute, but he knew he must keep digging. With bare hands he pulled snow out of the head's mouth and watched the person come to life. A faint smile crossed the face of Michel Desorbay as he looked up at Ang Tharkay and Bernard Pierre, who had just crawled over to help. Pierre had been powered by the strength of desperation, and as soon as he saw that Desorbay was alive, he fainted. Ang Tharkay continued to dig, and found to his horror that Desorbay was bent over backwards with the rope at his waist pulling his chest forward.

Pierre Vittoz watched the scene from above. When he saw two bodies come to the surface, he unroped and ran down the channel cut by the avalanche. Ang Tharkay and Bernard Pierre seemed to have only minor injuries, but Desorbay appeared to have a broken spine, which could be fatal at any moment. Vittoz helped Ang Tharkay dig Desorbay out. Soon the whole party assembled, including two Sherpas from Camp II who had witnessed the accident. To everyone's surprise, Desorbay's spine was pronounced intact by the doctor, and Desorbay was able to sit up and eventually to stand on his own. When this happened, Ang Tharkay finally collapsed and lay on the snow, moaning quietly. The doctor, Guillemin, checked him and found a number of contusions and some broken ribs. The Sherpas watched in amazement as Guillemin shot morphine into Ang Tharkay's thigh to stop a pain elsewhere in his body.

Soon the procession of climbers began to move down the mountain. Gloves and goggles had been lost in the chaos. The three avalanche victims, who were in constant pain, were kept on a tight rope from above. The group moved through the deep snows like a squadron of Napoleon's retreat from Moscow. The stop at Camp II was brief, for the doctor reasoned that further descent might not be possible if the morphine wore off and the weakened men allowed their injured muscles and joints to stiffen. That night they reached Camp I on the level plateau they had named "The Col of Good Hope." The next day they moved down to base camp, where earth, flowers, and an unlimited supply of water brought them back to the world of the living.

At base camp the expedition assessed its condition. The climb was scheduled to end in just five days, when the coolies would arrive for the long retreat march back to the Vale of Kashmir. The three avalanche victims were definitely out of action. All had broken ribs and multiple bruises. Ang Tharkay had the beginnings of pneumonia. Only Vittoz and Kogan had any chance of reaching the summit.

After a single rest day, a light and rapid summit bid began. Bernard Pierre felt as if someone were sticking a knife into his chest when he breathed hard, but he insisted on accompanying Vittoz and Kogan as high as he could go. With four Sherpas, the party reached Camp II in a single day. The next morning they headed for Camp III, but were turned back by zero visibility. The following morning they moved up in more reasonable weather, but they couldn't find the camp. The route looked unfamiliar, even though their altimeters indicated they were near the right spot. When the clouds cleared above them, they were startled to see that an enormous line of seracs had fallen from the summit ridge, burying Camp III without a trace. That meant that the three climbers and four Sherpas would all have to bivouac in a two-man tent they had with them, with no stove or water, so the party sent three of the four Sherpas back to Camp II.

The morning of August 28, 1953, came absolutely clear, and they started up the mountain. Bernard Pierre and Sherpa Pemba Nurbu soon turned back because of Pierre's injuries. Kogan and Vittoz kept going, using ski poles to wade through the deep snow left by the long storms. The final windblown ridge rose at a constant fifty degrees toward the sky. The air was clear and still. They had plenty of physical reserves, and conditions for making the summit seemed perfect except for one thing: avalanche. They recognized with horror the same conditions that had caused the accident just five days before on a more gentle slope.

Acoustics in the mountains can be amazingly good. In the tent at Camp III, Pierre clearly heard Kogan ask Vittoz, "Shall we go on?" Vittoz said simply, "Yes; let's."

His thoughts were more complex. He constantly glanced downward toward the security of the lower camps, wondering if the summit of Nun was worth the risk they were taking. He had become fascinated by his increasing ability to judge whether the snow was safe by the single kick of his heavy boot. He moved through an ever-changing element, sometimes deciding to go straight up so as not to cut the slope, other times veering sideways to avoid an island of dangerous windslab. He and Kogan became sailors in a sea of snow, rising on the crest of a high wave. They were surrounded by a turbulent ocean of whitecaps, isolated from humanity by choice.

Life became starkly simple. They tried to reach the summit and stay alive. They divided the work of kicking steps equally by changing the lead at each rope's length. This rhythm of effort and rest, concentration and random thought, continued until Kogan yelled down, "Come along; the last few yards are wide enough for us to go together."

They stayed on the summit for a brief half hour, knowing that there would be no success unless they could get back to Camp III that day. Far to the west a curtain shimmered above the other whitecaps, turned yellow by the haze. This was Nanga Parbat, rising from the Indus River in a 23,000-foot thrust. To the northwest was a row of sharp pyramids on the skyline, aligned like teeth in the jaw of a shark. These were the six summits over 26,000 feet in the Karakoram Himalaya, 125 miles away. To the east was the Garwhal Himalaya, dominated by Kamet and Nanda Devi. Between them and these great peaks there were no peaks higher than their own. For more than 400 miles along the crest of the Greater Himalaya, Nun Kun reigned supreme. The view from its summit gave a feeling of height and isolation equal to that from Everest itself.

Ang Tharkay never gained that view. He had watched with melancholy resignation as Vittoz headed back up the mountain. When the summit was reached, Ang Tharkay was in Base camp, thinking of his wife and four daughters in Darjeeling and the long and painful march home.

3 | Through Kashmir to Ladakh

Dawn in Delhi. At five in the morning six of us had burst out of the hotel in shorts, without shirts, to get some exercise after the long flight. Tim, the marathoner, set the pace. Malcolm, Gus, Maynard, Kim, and I followed. The temperature and humidity were both nearly one hundred as we ran through the streets. In the section of New Delhi where our early morning run began, the wide streets and spacious mansions reflected years of British rule. The district bore little resemblance to Old Delhi, where each house was connected to an endless row, and each person belonged to a flowing river of humanity. We were on a cultural island. It had been built up in the previous century during the British Raj and had been reconnected to the mainland by independence in 1947. Mansions that once housed British officers now belonged to Indian businessmen. The streets were nearly empty, except for an occasional bicycle, horsecart, or taxi.

We jogged past a palace, past the parliament buildings, and eventually we reached a business district. Doors were just opening and people were beginning to fill the streets.

Suddenly we were no longer passive observers; our presence influenced those around us. Street people dressed in ragged *dhotis* and sandals were awestruck by the sight of a phalanx of nearly naked Americans. To them we were huge, muscular creatures engaged in an activity they couldn't com-

Sunrise over Dal Lake, Vale of Kashmir

prehend. Unwittingly, we were flaunting our wealth even though we were wearing almost nothing. To people who survived on less than 1,000 calories a day, running for exercise was unknown. Like us Americans, they were involved in an energy crisis, but the fuel they craved was for their own bodies, not for machines. Lower caste Indians spend over eighty percent of their incomes for food.

The smiles we had seen from a distance disappeared as we drew near. We had come on them too suddenly in a way that was somehow threatening. Back in our luxury hotel we felt quite self-conscious.

Later in the morning we set out to secure government permission for our expedition. To those unfamiliar with Asian ways, the process seemed disarmingly simple. All we had to do was present ourselves at the visa office with a letter from the Indian Embassy in the United States. Renee Chandola, the young Indian woman who managed Mountain Travel, India, had set aside the entire day, if necessary, to help secure the approval of our visas. We appeared in person with her at a government office where a long row of men sat behind a table. Each one had to read, approve, stamp, and sign each application. A wrong answer on a form, like a speck of grit in a machine, ground the process to a halt. When one of the officials discovered an error—such as the wrong city listed under "Place of Disembarkation"—all work ceased until it was resolved. Renee patiently oiled the gears of the bureaucracy with a steady application of charm, wit, and feminine wiles backed by thorough preparation. Educated as she was in England and South Africa, Renee Chandola fully understood the differences between India and the Western world. When climbers who had never been to Asia commented on the slowness of the process, Renee replied lightly, "We're all on Eastern Standard Time here." In just two hours—a relative Asian instant—we walked out the door with our visas in hand.

After two days of sightseeing and equipment-gathering in Delhi, we flew to Srinigar. The eighty-five-mile-long Vale of Kashmir looked like a giant slab of jade set into the snow-covered mountains. As we drove to town from the airport at sunset, I thought I had never seen a more beautiful setting for a city. Roads and canals were lined with poplars, and every piece of flat land was green with planted rice. Much of the population lived in houseboats on the waters of the canals and the two large lakes, Dal and Wular. Shikaras, the Kashmiri versions of gondolas, were not only means of transport, but were also floating markets, pharmacies, and post offices. We were somewhat disappointed when we reached the center of town. Compared to Kathmandu at a similar elevation in Nepal, the inner city was squalid, ramshackle, and undistinguished. We felt as if we had come upon Tenement City in the middle of Jackson Hole, Wyoming.

After dinner, Kim and I went out on the town with Rich Nowack. We were drawn to a great mosque by the bank of the Jhelum River, where a continuous flow of people moved in and out of the building, but never by the front door. When we investigated, we were invited into the basement by a man with eyes as hazy as the air of a bazaar. There we found forty-odd men in a circle puffing on water pipes, each with eyes like the first man's. We had stumbled into a hash parlor. An hour later we more literally stumbled back to the street with Rich clutching a fist-sized piece of hashish as if it were the Hope diamond. It had cost him four dollars.

The next day, Chris LaRocca, the last member of our expedition, arrived and we were ready to go. The group was eager to reach the mountain as soon as possible. Dirt roads built after the Chinese invasion of Ladakh in 1962 led two hundred miles to the very base of the mountain. Because of slow mountain passes, the trip would take two days. From the rice paddies of the Vale we climbed a gorge lined with lush meadows and forest until the legendary Zoji La came into view. The 11,578-foot pass was at the top of a long series of switchbacks etched into a high cliff.

Long before the road had been constructed, Himalayan traders had used this route during the few months each year when it was free of snow. Now we saw an amazing tableau of humanity, moving against a backdrop of snow, cloud, forest, and sky. Nomads with pack animals, looking straight out of the days of Ghengis Khan, alternated with hundreds of Shaktiman four-wheel-drive army trucks that convoyed goods to forty thousand Indian soldiers stationed in the highlands. Jam-packed public buses and trucks honked their way past families herding goats, cattle, and horses to summer pasture in Ladakh.

On the other side of the pass we went through the bleak village of Dras, reportedly the second coldest place in Asia with recorded temperatures of -80°F. Kargil was a bustling Moslem town with only a hint of the Buddhism that was prevalent in the higher mountains. As we ascended into the Suru Valley, we saw fewer dark and slender Kashmiris and more Mongol faces with occasional blue eyes and light-colored skin. According to legend, these highlands above the Indus River Valley were populated with descendants from the army of Alexander the Great, who had passed to the south in 327 B.C. From that same campaign comes one of the earliest descriptions of technical climbing. Alexander wanted to capture a high rock in the Himalayan foothills where his enemies had taken refuge. It was vertical on all sides and coated with snow and ice. He offered a large prize to the first men on top. His biographer, Arrian, wrote the following description:

"There were some three hundred men who in previous sieges had had experience in rock-climbing. These now assembled. They had provided themselves with small iron tent-pegs, which they proposed to drive into the snow where it was frozen hard . . . and they had attached to the pegs strong flaxen lines. They set off under the cover of darkness to the steepest part of the rockface . . . then, driving their pegs either into bare ground or into such patches of snow as seemed most likely to hold under the strain, they hauled themselves up."

Where Alexander's techniques originated and what became of them remains a mystery. None of the region's mountain people today use ropes or climb especially difficult terrain.

Unlike the Sherpa people of the Mount Everest region, the people of Tangul, the tiny village at 11,500 feet below Nun Kun, had no tradition of serving climbing expeditions. We found that Sylvain Saudan had arrived in Tangul before us and had hired the most able porters. We were left with thirty of the very young and the very old.

At our Tangul camp, everyone was in good humor. Tents were pitched in a rock-strewn field directly under steep slopes leading to base camp, only three hours' walk away. Evening light intensified the green of the fields and the depth of the Suru River gorge, which curved off into a semicircle of snowy peaks. Rich had come running into camp the previous evening after smoking some of his Srinigar windfall. All eyes were on him as he danced through the rocks with arms outstretched and feet barely touching the ground, announcing, "I have just experienced the moments of creation."

The next day we established base camp at 13,500 feet in a snow-filled basin. Major Kumar did a fine job of managing the porters, and Mridula, his sister-in-law, cooked one of the best meals I had ever eaten in the mountains. The Kumars assured us that Sherpas were on the way to us, but we didn't dare count on their help until they arrived in the flesh. Too many assurances had already proved false: the major's brother, Colonel Narinder Kumar, had gone to a different mountain, the "Ladakhi Sherpas" had quit, plus we had a desperate shortage of tents, no emergency oxygen, no walkie-talkies, and no high-altitude stoves or cook sets.

In the evening I gathered people together and explained our shortages. Most were already known, but I thought a public clearing of the air would do some good. A few of the Tangul villagers could carry loads to an ice plateau at 17,000 feet, but beyond that point we would be entirely on our own unless the Nepalese Sherpas arrived. I was gratified to hear that all of the paying clients were more than willing to begin carrying loads with the porters to make the expedition a success. I invited anyone who questioned any of my decisions to ask me about them. They might well have a better idea, and it would promote better understanding to talk about it. I also asked that tent partners be shifted every few days, both for people to know each other better, and for avoiding strong factions that might operate outside the group. There would be no leader's tent; Kim and I planned to rotate tent berths with the others. On the lower mountain we would move slowly, waiting three days to advance into each camp so as to avoid altitude sickness. On the upper mountain, however, we might be forced into an alpine-style push if Sherpa support and additional tents failed to arrive.

The following morning we began ferrying loads to an advanced base camp at 16,200 feet. There we found Sylvain Saudan ensconced in luxury with folding chairs and a portable liquor closet. We set up camp about a hundred yards away—close enough to be neighbors ,but far enough apart to maintain some solitude. It took three days to move all our goods, and when we finally had everything in the higher camp the weather closed in and it began to snow. There was no despondency over this turn of events, for we had already weathered other crises of equipment and promised support. The adversities seemed to draw us closer to one another; I had yet to hear a single harsh word directed at another person. A couple of the team members had showed themselves to be eccentric, but instead of shunning and rejecting them, the group put out extra effort to draw them into the circle.

Upper right
Women in a rice paddy, Vale of Kashmir
Right
Hash parlor in the basement of a mosque, Srinigar.

Left
Srinigar, Kashmir
Lower left
Meadows on the Kashmiri side of the Zoji La

That evening Kim and I drew up a schedule of eleven to fifteen days for climbing the mountain. If tents and Sherpas didn't arrive, we would rush the upper part of the mountain—but not before the group had a solid base of acclimatization and a well-stocked camp on the ice plateau. We would still spend at least three days each at the next two camps before moving higher.

We found it hard to discuss the plan seriously with the group because everyone was trying to be lighthearted. Maynard said that he would eat the entire bottle of spicy chutney that happened to be in his hand if he got to the summit in fifteen days. We were all anxious about the climb, and Maynard's aside offered a welcome opportunity to turn the conversation toward food. That night we were eating our first heavy meat dinner, supposedly from a sheep that had been led up to base camp. Pat, noticing that Mrs. Kumar's high-strung German shepherd had not come to our advanced base, asked, "Has anybody seen the dog lately?" Mrs. Kumar, in turn, took me to the side to tell me her concern for Bernie Najaka, who refused to eat her mildly seasoned cooking and survived almost entirely on eggs. With his large biceps, New Jersey accent, and vast consumption of eggs, Bernie had earned the affectionate nickname of "Rocky." "What will we do?" Mrs. Kumar asked. "We're almost out of eggs even though we brought three crates of chickens to Tangul." I hoped that Bernie would eat the freeze-dried rations that we would use above 17,000 feet.

As snow blanketed the camp, Gus Benner played his harmonica and Bernie spewed a stream of one-liners like a veteran comedian. I wrote the following entry in my diary: "Perhaps a mail-order Himalayan expedition resembles an Asian marriage, where a couple doesn't meet until their wedding, but has better odds of getting along than a Western couple who marry after months or years of tested compatibility."

Guiding at 23,000 Feet

Only fifteen minutes after we had returned from carrying loads to 17,500 feet, a block of ice fell from a cliff far to the left of our route. It triggered a massive slide of fresh snow that diagonaled for hundreds of yards across the almost-level glacier, wiping out our tracks and leaving the surface of the glacier lumpy, with the appearance of cottage cheese.

The event forced us to reassess our attitude toward the mountain. Our own humor and Saudan's nonchalance had led us to consider it a big, benevolent giant. We almost forgot that Saudan had failed to reach the summit a year before, when the route that was now snow had been a jumble of ice.

A city of a hundred thousand people could have fit easily on the Great Ice Plateau at 17,500 feet. We chose to camp near Saudan in the lee of a snow hill. Both our expeditions had been using a few of the strongest Tangul porters up to this point, but neither had a single porter who would venture higher. Temperatures had already dipped below zero Fahrenheit, and we were thankful that the Tangulis had come this far in their Indian-made plastic oxfords. While we dined on freeze-dried franks and beans, Saudan had an entirely different diet. He owned a restaurant called L'Impossible, and he had brought his chef, Andre Chaucheprat, to cook delicacies for the expedition. Kim and I were invited to Saudan's camp and were served wine, cheese, and caviar from a table straight

The Great Ice Plateau at 17,500 feet on Nun

out of a travel advertisement. In our camp, we cooked in a floorless cotton tent similar to those used in the lowlands by turn-of-the-century explorers.

On the ninth day above base, the arrival of four men with Mongol features changed the entire mood of the expedition. The Sherpas had come! As soon as they put down their loads they set about making a new kitchen, complete with a sunken table cut into the snow. Their whole beings seemed focused on our needs, yet they lost nothing of their individuality in the process. Ajiwa, a roly-poly fellow in his early twenties, constantly laughed and joked. Ang Tsering, a slender fellow about the same age, was tolerant of the gaity, but with an aloof, inquiring attitude that reminded me of Heinrich Harrer's description of the young Dalai Lama. Both the other men were named Gyalzen: one was young and stocky, while the other was a sinewy old man who could have passed for the younger man's grandfather. Ang Tsering was the only one who could converse with us by means of very limited English.

The morning after the Sherpas came, I noticed that they were shivering as they served us tea and biscuits in our tents at 6:00 A.M. They wore only light hiking shoes and thin jackets. They had absolutely no high-altitude equipment, and they had never been to Ladakh before. For them to help us stock a higher camp, they would need boots, parkas, ice axes, and tents. Only three would go higher in any event, because old Gyalzen had ceased high-altitude work after losing two relatives on Mount Everest. When Major Kumar, who had never been on a big peak in his life, unexpectedly appeared in plateau camp with two Tangul porters, we asked if there was any point in waiting for more equipment to arrive. His answer was not encouraging. He explained that the Sherpas had rushed to join us from a hiking trek, and that telegrams to Delhi and Srinigar had not produced a single tent or item of clothing.

A reconnaissance to the base of the French route brought back more grim information. Fresh avalanches crossed the route, and because the route was quite indirect—winding over a rock tower and through a jumble of seracs—it would definitely require two additional camps. With our tent shortage, the best we could manage would be one more camp. Several of our America-made dome tents were already crippled by a rash of broken poles. We had not a single two-man mountain tent, and we feared that a high wind would destroy any dome tent used in an exposed position.

On the plus side of the ledger, our entire team of fifteen climbers was at 17,500 feet and was healthy. The slow pace and long acclimatization had paid good dividends, but without tentage or logistical support, we certainly couldn't go higher except for a very short time.

At first I had considered the Czech route on the northwest ridge to be out of the question. The Czechs had succeeded on that route, where a Japanese expedition had failed before them, only by placing five thousand feet of fixed rope over steep rock and ice. I saw another possible line that would follow the Czech ridge to 20,000 feet and then traverse the unclimbed west face until it hit the French ridge just below the 23,410-foot summit. It was very direct, and I thought that Kim and I could do it alpine-style with only one camp. The important question was: could we consider those tactics with clients?

The weather was unstable, and we wanted to spend some days acclimatizing on the plateau before moving higher. The clients themselves strongly influenced the course of events. Larry got together a work crew to dig a large snow cave that could serve as a shelter if anything happened to our tents

Night in base camp at 13,500 feet on Nun Kun massif

above. Tom made a strong case for trying the Czech ridge rather than the French route. Several people volunteered to lend their clothing, boots, and axes to the Sherpas if they weren't chosen to go on the first summit bid.

When we did formulate a plan, Bernie made the greatest sacrifice of all. Instead of saving himself for a summit bid, he offered to carry loads with the Sherpas to increase our odds of success. If we did succeed in forging a climbable route, we would organize further summit tries for the remainder of the team.

Six climbers began a push for the summit at 4:00 A.M. on June 17. The strongest and most experienced had been chosen to attempt a semialpine-style ascent of the unclimbed west face. On my rope were Maynard Cohick and Peter Cummings. On Kim's were Gus Benner and Pat O'Donnell. Two of the three-man dome tents would go with us to a camp at 20,500 feet, from where the unequipped Sherpas would descend for the night. The fifty-pound loads were difficult to manage on a 3,000-foot day over untracked ground at altitude, but they would have been heavier had it not been for Bernie's help.

At first we walked through ankle-deep snow at a moderate angle. Then we encountered powder up to our thighs. We alternated breaking trail for hours until we reached the crest and found where the deep snow had come from. Wind had blown all the fresh snow to the lee side, leaving the crest capped with hard ice. The only feasible campsite was on a twenty-degree slope, where we spent three hours chopping with ice axes before the round tents could be set up on lumpy, slanting platforms and tied in to ice screws. The effort of digging at over 20,000 feet was far greater than that of climbing. Sweating and rapid breathing gave way to shivering when we stopped for a rest.

The weather had closed in as we concentrated on setting up camp, and an hour before sunset it began to snow. Bernie and the Sherpas headed down at a rapid pace to get back to the plateau by dark, leaving the six of us alone in the storm with two days of food. I guessed that we would be forced to descend the next day.

At 4:30 A.M., long before the sun actually rose, I peered out of the tent and saw Nun's immense shadow cast against a clear sky. A blue blanket seemed to cover an endless vista of snowy whitecaps. As I watched, the top of a distant pyramid to the west turned pink, and I recognized K2, the second highest mountain in the world. Then other summits began to glow in the sunrise. Like attendants in front of their king, the pointed tops of the four Gasherbrums—all over 26,000 feet—surrounded K2. To the south of them, Masherbrum thrust a symmetrical cone into the dawn's light. Hidden behind Masherbrum were the Trango Towers, 125 air miles away.

Most impressive of all was Nanga Parbat, thrusting miles of icy tapestry into the sky. Here was the highest exposed land escarpment on earth—23,000 feet of mountain rising out of the Indus River Gorge. Farther back to the right was Rakaposhi, 25,000-foot giant of the kingdom of Hunza. Even when the alpenglow ended, the great peaks stood out from the myriad of white mountains in front of them as if they were lit by an amber stage light, because their greater distance gave the snow a distinctive hue.

To our great joy, there was not a cloud in the sky. After we had consumed our cocoa, tea, and oatmeal, the six of us headed toward the summit wearing heavy clothing for the subzero conditions and crampons on our boots. A few hundred feet above camp we passed the bare blue top of an ice hummock by walking onto a cornice that overhung the Ganri Glacier, thousands of feet below. I left one of our two extra ropes fixed to safeguard the descent and traversed out onto the unclimbed west face.

In powdery and unconsolidated snow, we step-plugged up a gradual slope that soon steepened to forty degrees under the rock ridge that the Czechs had climbed. The other climbers who had alternated breaking trail with Kim and me at lower altitudes could not hold the pace up high. Checking our progress, I wondered if we would make the top. Only Kim seemed fit enough to switch into the lead, but his rope of three was not keeping up with mine. I kept moving at an even tempo, first kicking a step into the soft snow, then putting my weight onto it and sinking down within inches of the height of my other boot. There was no skill involved here, other than facing a task not unlike shoveling the longest driveway in the world.

We lunched in the sun on a rock shelf at nearly 22,500 feet. It was one o'clock, and by simple arithmetic, the final 900 feet would take about two hours. However, we had not only fatigue and increasing elevation to contend with, but also a long horizontal traverse over an area where the snow was suspiciously dark. Billowing cumulus clouds were building rapidly, and by 2:30 P.M. we were front-pointing across hard ice in a snowstorm. The angle was a steady fifty-five degrees with bulges that were even steeper. At one of these spots, Peter took a fall, but was held by the rope attached to an ice screw. When he tried to climb back up, he discovered that he had slipped over a horizontal crevasse. He was able to traverse to a point where he could step over the hole, but he questioned whether we should continue, saying that the steep ice and exposure were more than he had bargained for. I agreed, but suggested that we climb another hundred feet to a rock escarpment. From there we could see the conditions above. I ran out the rope to a ledge, and saw easier climbing ahead. I placed a piton to secure a handline for the others. Peter came up without hesitation, but Maynard moved very slowly, taking half an hour to work up the rope with a Jumar ascender. I kept thinking that if I hadn't placed the rope at all, Maynard would have managed the spot handily with just ice axe and crampons. Adding technical gear—ropes, pitons, and Jumars—at high altitude was mind-boggling to anyone who wasn't so familiar with the gear's use that he could handle it blindfolded at sea level.

Meanwhile, Kim, Pat, and Gus stopped below. Through the blizzard Kim could only distinguish Maynard's dark form spending a very long time on a fixed rope. He couldn't see the terrain clearly, and he assumed that the climbing was extreme. He yelled for us to throw down the rope as soon as Maynard was up. I answered that he didn't need the rope, but the wind was against me and Kim couldn't hear a word. Finally we threw one end down to Kim, but he didn't make a move to get it.

Our effort was coming apart. Kim's group did not seem to be in trouble, yet they were making no motions to come up to us. It was 4:30—my predetermined turn-around time. Not being able to communicate with Kim, I simply had to trust him to do the right thing. I turned to Maynard and Peter and said, "We've got three choices now. First, we can go on like we are, but we'll have to turn around before the top. Second, we can turn back now. Third, we can dress with everything we have, leave our packs, cameras, and extra gear attached to this piton, and go for it. There is no other way we can make these last five hundred feet and get down before nightfall."

Maynard talked about going down. He said that the climbers below were our primary responsibility. I agreed with him that our responsibility for safety came far ahead of anyone's desire for the summit, but I asked what he thought we could do for the others? Kim was an excellent leader and they did not appear to be in any trouble. The only problem was that they had ceased moving up. We could no longer understand them, and if they made no effort to climb the fixed rope, then we were free to continue. Our two ropes of three could move just as safely as a line of six. I pulled up the rope while Kim watched and made no motion for us to come down.

Minutes later I was leading upward on a ridge crest of firm snow. The wind gusted to sixty knots, but inside our parkas and overpants we were warm. Hard ice had been a serious problem; now only snow stretched out of sight into the sky. Visibility had been less than the length of our rope; now occasional blue patches opened overhead. And our bodies, fatigued from six thousand feet of climbing in two days, still seemed to have some reserves left. While moving with a group on a mountain, I often let my mind wander to home, to loved ones, to another mountain or to solve some meaningless little problem. Now I didn't dare think that way. My thoughts were totally concerned with monitoring our progress. I had to be ready to turn back if our last-ditch effort was too slow. First came a false summit; then another. Finally I could go no higher and as I stood in a windy fury, a patch of blue sky appeared overhead. For a moment it cleared all around me and evening light shone on an endless panorama of peaks. Far to the east I could make out Nanda Devi and the Garwhal Himalaya. To the west I caught a glimpse of Nanga Parbat, but my view of it lasted less than a minute. Falling snow blew by me in a sinewy flow that reminded me of watching a waterfall. I was standing in one of the summit plumes that we had so often admired from below. I stepped down from the tiny summit so that Peter could move up. When it became Maynard's turn we had trouble getting him to come down. He wanted to savor the moments that had taken him so much effort to attain.

Half an hour later we got back to our packs and were surprised to find the others waiting on the ledge in a raging blizzard. They had climbed slightly higher before giving up the effort and waiting for us to return. Soon we recrossed the ice face, but the fatigue of pushing for the top had caught up to our threesome.

Kim's group outdistanced us, and within the hour we were alone in the storm, following tracks that were rapidly filling in with blowing snow. Then came the most amazing light I ever saw on a mountain. Through the surrounding grayness a pink glow came up underneath us, backlighting our forms and making us seem as if we were floating through the sky. Here was the direct opposite of a conventional sunset; darkness was above the horizon and the red glow was at our feet. We were in a local storm while the lower mountain was clear. The glow of the sun's last rays was hitting snow slopes below us. The lower we climbed, the brighter and clearer the display became.

I wanted so much to stop the group and take photos, but I knew that to do so would break the rhythm of our descent, just as a piton and a fixed rope had taken undue time away from the ascent. I was worried about descending the ice bulge just above camp after dark.

When we broke out of the storm, darkness was already upon us. A crescent moon helped us follow tracks until we neared the ice bulge after 9:00 P.M. Normally a guide goes last on the descent to hold a possible slip, but here I elected to go first, navigating by tapping the edge of the cornice with my ice axe in an outstretched hand in order to stay back from the edge. A few feet in from the edge was bare ice, and I breathed a sigh of relief when my hand touched the fixed rope I had placed in the morning. We rappelled down and reached camp just after 10:00 P.M., where the others were snug in their sleeping bags.

We parted company the next morning and I led four of us down to the ice plateau. Kim stayed in high camp with Pat to make another bid for the top. They would rest a day, while I went down to send up others. I had the plateau camp moved to a rocky spur directly below the route. Anyone who wanted to join the next summit bid was to be packed and waiting when we arrived. About midmorning, we walked into the open arms of our comrades. Our lives seemed completely fulfilled as we sat on warm rocks, drank hot tea, and told of our adventure. Maynard and Peter talked about the rigors of the ascent, but Gus's simple story had greater effect on the group. He told of pushing hard all day and missing the summit by a few hundred feet. Here was Gus, the most steady and selfless of the group and among its strongest, saying that he wasn't going to make another try.

Only three people showed interest in making a second dash for the top. Tim was the strongest of the clients, but he had declined to join the first bid. Now he was ready to go. Larry had told the others he wanted to go, but he had left camp without leaving word when he would return. We couldn't wait for him, because whoever was chosen to go would have to make high camp by evening. Malcolm wanted to go very badly, but I told him that he didn't have the experience to handle the ice traverse. He could go to high camp with Tim, but he should make it clear to Kim that I had not sent him as a summit climber. Within the hour, Tim, Malcolm, and two Sherpas were on their way up. Later in the day, Tim came down, having decided not to take the risk. Malcolm continued.

June 20 dawned clear. We watched three people leave high camp at 6:30 A.M.—an hour and a half earlier than on the first summit bid. From our plateau camp, Norm, Tom, Chris, and Larry headed up to high camp for a day trip. The rest of us lay shirtless on flat, warm slabs of black slate. At first the summit party made faster progress than we had. Then they slowed down on the ice traverse and only two moved toward the top from the rocks where we had cached our packs. We cheered when they reached the summit, but began to worry when their downward progress was exceedingly slow and one climber moved quite erratically. Darkness overtook them long before they reached camp. How I wished we had the walkie-talkies that had never arrived!

I went to Ang Tsering and tried to impress on him the gravity of the situation. I asked him to leave at first light with the other two Sherpas and go as quickly as possible to high camp. If they found no one there, they should go as high as they safely could to locate and assist the returning summit party.

At 10:30 that night Rich awoke me, saying he had heared muffled screams in the distance. I listened for a while and heard nothing. At 4:30 A.M. I awoke to another voice just outside the tent. Ang Tsering was saying, "Chai, sahib!"

I instantly felt guilty. The Sherpas were in their crampons and ready to go on a mission we had said could mean life or death, but they had prepared tea and breakfast for us! I had forgotten to tell them that they needn't bother with normal tasks during the emergency. Rather than question my instructions, however, they had gotten up an hour earlier to cook for us. As we sipped hot

Upper left
Sunset from high on Nun
Left
*The shadow of Nun cast
into the stratosphere
by predawn light
from high camp at
20,500 feet.*
Above
*The Karakoram Range from
Nun Kun; K2 in center.*
Right
*Traversing under the
summit ridge on Nun at
22,000 feet.*

tea in our warm bags, we occasionally peered out to watch them move up the steep snow at tremendous speed. It had taken us nine hours with loads to reach the 20,500-foot camp, but the Sherpas made it in an hour and forty minutes. As they neared the camp, sun struck the tents and one person stood profiled against the sky. Then came another, and a third. All three climbers were in high camp.

Later that day the expedition was all together again, and I learned how close we had come to tragedy. Malcolm had taken Tim's place on the rope of three, and he had considerable difficulty with the ice traverse. When a piece broke on his crampon, he stayed behind on a ledge while Kim and Pat went to the top. On the descent Malcolm took many falls because of his broken crampon, fatigue, and inexperience. Pat and Kim kept him on a tight rope between them. As they headed down the final slope in the darkness, Kim went first to navigate between the cornice and the ice to find the fixed rope placed two days earlier. When he located it, he reset the ice screws that had been loosened by the sun and descended slowly, using the fixed rope as a handline.

As he neared the end of the rope, he heard scuffling above him followed by a noise that he recognized: the jingle of climbing hardware that was temporarily weightless during free fall. He was standing on blue ice, and when he blindly tried to sink in his axe, it glanced off the surface. In desperation—with only seconds before the climbing rope would come tight—Kim kicked in his front points, leaned into the wall, and wrapped the fixed rope once around his arm.

A tremendous jerk came; Kim held it. An even stronger one followed, and somehow he remained standing, holding two ropes that seemed stretched to their absolute limits, with his four crampon front points sunk more firmly than ever into the slope.

The fall had come in an instant. The tight climbing rope from Kim to Malcolm to Pat had jerked Pat from his tracks; Pat fell, he pulled Malcolm down, and the two of them went down the slope. When they reached the end of the climbing rope, Kim held a 200-foot fall with two men on the rope and all three men were unhurt.

We held a meeting and decided that our assault on the mountain was over. No one else wanted to try the summit under the existing conditions. With extra tents and equipment, we could have made the route climbable for the entire expedition, but there was great satisfaction in what had already been achieved by this first American commercial expedition to a peak over 7,000 meters. Five of us had reached the summit and all but two out of fifteen had reached 20,000 feet. We had no serious injuries or illnesses, and not a single voice had been raised in anger toward another team member.

We stayed an extra day on the plateau, waiting to watch Saudan reach the summit and ski down, but his party failed to reach the summit by just a few hundred feet. We descended to base camp and found grass and wildflowers where there had been snow three weeks before. Abdul Rashid, our government liaison officer, took me aside to ask about a strange animal he had seen in base camp the previous evening. It was a cat as large as a goat with a long tail. I said, "Rashid, you've seen a snow leopard!"

"No!" he said emphatically. "A snow leopard would have attacked us!" I questioned him extensively and learned that the animal had circled the camp at dusk at a distance of fifty yards. Only Rashid and the cook were present, and the cook said that he had seen the same animal a day earlier. It was tawny, large, spotted, long-tailed, and definitely a cat, but Rashid was certain it couldn't have been a snow leopard. When I found large cat tracks outside camp, I was even more certain that Rashid had indeed seen one of the rarest and most beautiful of the world's big cats. I wrote in my diary, "Incredible! I'd rather have seen a snow leopard than have climbed Nun."

After a rest day in base camp, we continued our descent through a dreamland of green hillsides decorated with cascading streams and bright flowers. We felt as if we were traveling in a time machine as we experienced winter on the Great Ice Plateau, found spring on the lower slopes, and entered the heat of summer in the Vale of Kashmir. There we spent two days relaxing and celebrating.

On the day we arrived in the Vale, Saudan reached the top of Nun and skied down. It took him four hours and nearly 3,000 turns to negotiate the 7,000 feet of the upper mountain—turning endlessly on windblown snow and ice, jumping crevasses, and dodging rock outcrops. His joy was different from ours, but each of us felt that we shared some of it. We had been on the same mountain together and weathered the same storms. For Saudan and for each of the clients, Nun Kun had provided the adventure of the year—perhaps the adventure of a lifetime.

5 | The Coming of Age of Adventure Travel

In 1950, Mount Everest began its transformation of an unclimbed mountain with unknown southern approaches into a tourist attraction inside a new national park where annual visitors outnumber Sherpa residents by more than two to one. The mountain straddles the border between Tibet and Nepal. In 1950, Tibet suddenly closed after an invasion by the Chinese Army, while Nepal ended a century of seclusion by opening her borders to foreigners.

Both the region and its people have a timeless, immutable quality. They seem, like ancient oriental art, to be something out of a mystical world beyond change. It is hard to reconcile this illusion with the reality of rapid geological and cultural alteration. So young are the Himalaya mountains that during the rise of the human race late in the Pleistocene Epoch, Mount Everest gained at least half its present altitude. Jumbo jets filled with tourists now cruise eye-to-eye with Everest; the first flight of the Wright brothers seventy-five years ago did not reach the height of a parked 747's cockpit. Changes in the last twenty-five years, however, have made even more difference than the advent of flight. An infrared photograph made from a satellite in 1974 shows a new 40,000-square-mile island about to surface in the Bay of Bengal. The island is the

Trekkers' lunch stop in the Khumbu region of Nepal

product of Nepal's unwitting export of topsoil down the Ganges River; deforestation and overuse of hill tracts is to blame.

By gearing their economy toward tourism, the Sherpa people of the Everest region have staved off some of the pitfalls that have befallen their neighbors. What the future holds for them can best be predicted by tracing how they came to the position they hold today.

Until 1950, no Westerner had traveled through the homeland of the Sherpas to the base of Mount Everest. Isolated from all visitors by their nation's politics, the Sherpas became known to explorers and climbers only because some of them traveled to Darjeeling in India to look for work around the turn of the century. A research chemist from London, Dr. A.M. Kellas, trained some Darjeeling coolies and rickshaw-wallahs as mountain porters for his expedition in 1907 to a minor peak near the Nepal border. He discovered that certain men were far better suited to the task than others, and it could hardly be coincidence that all these men were from the Sherpa tribe, which constituted only a fraction of a percent of Nepal's population.

It would be impossible to imagine people whose lifestyle was more compatible with becoming mountain porters and guides. The name Sherpa means "people from the east," and about four centuries ago they migrated across high passes from Tibet into uninhabited valleys on the Nepal side of Mount Everest. Their villages in the Khumbu Valley lie at an average elevation of 13,000 feet—far too high for dependable subsistence farming until the introduction of the potato, late in the nineteenth century. These seminomadic people supplemented the yields of their short growing season by herding yaks in high summer pastures and managing the salt trade between Tibet and the Nepalese lowlands. Their Mahayana Buddhist teachings—unlike those of Hindus and Moslems in other parts of the Himalaya—allowed them to live and work freely and cheerfully with unbelievers.

Contrary to the myth perpetuated by many history books, the first Western visitors to the Khumbu did not come just to reconnoiter climbing possibilities on Mount Everest. They were true forerunners of a time when thousands of trekkers would walk through the Khumbu for the simple joy of being there. The first group's leader, Oscar Houston, was a 67-year-old doctor who came to Nepal in the autumn of 1950 as a guest of the Rana Maharajah in Kathmandu. During the course of his month's visit he unexpectedly received permission to travel in the Khumbu.

Oscar Houston cabled three other Americans to join him: Elizabeth Cowles, the Rev. Anderson Bakewell, and his son, Dr. Charles Houston, who had led expeditions to K2 and Nanda Devi before the war. Bill Tilman, who had led a 1938 Everest attempt from the Tibetan side and was fresh from a reconnaissance of Annapurna, joined the expedition on the eve of its departure. Oscar Houston, a great outdoor lover rather than an expeditionary mountaineer, certainly wanted to see if Everest looked climbable from Nepal, but the fact that leaders of expeditions to the world's two highest mountains were members of the party was an accident.

The Houston party was in Asia at a time when the governments of the noncommunist world discouraged tourism there, because of the very real fear that the entire subcontinent might fall to the communists by the end of the year. The Korean War had erupted, and the Chinese had invaded Tibet. While the party made its way on foot from Jogbani on the Indian frontier toward the heart of the Khumbu, a revolution ended Nepal's longstanding Rana regime. Houston's party stepped out of these black clouds of unrest into a land where they were constantly invited in for tea, smiled at, laughed at, touched, and given simple gifts. Luck was with them, and the new government in Kathmandu decided to continue the Rana policy allowing mountain tourism.

Only Tilman and the younger Houston walked all the way to the base of Everest, and they returned to the others at Thyangboche Monastery with considerable disappointment over the lack of a safe route to the South Col. An icefall, which has since claimed the lives of seventeen Sherpas in the process of getting twelve expeditions to the summit, appeared too dangerous for their style of lightweight expedition.

As the Houston party hiked out of the Khumbu on well-maintained trails that showed no sign of overuse, the only hint that the route had been walked for centuries came from polished cobblestones and coatings of lichens on rock carvings. Charles and Oscar Houston differed somewhat on the portent of their visit. The younger man, Charles, hoped for improvements in health and education; his father, Oscar, did not want the government to penetrate a land so untouched by progress. Father turned to son and said, "After we tell the world about this place, it will never be the same, and if we don't, another party will come soon and they will tell what they found." But Charles remained optimistic. High-altitude tourism did not exist then, and he foresaw future visitors like himself: dedicated climbers or scientists who would want to preserve the region's beauty. The real consequences of his visit, like the side effects of the new drugs in his medical kit, would not show for many years. Tilman sided with Oscar Houston in being skeptical about the effects of opening Nepal.

Tourism in Nepal started slowly. Indian National Airways began scheduled service to Kathmandu in 1951, but Nepal was not on the itinerary of even a standard tour group until March 1955, when members of a Thos. Cook and Sons round-the-world cruise flew in from Calcutta for a two-night stay.

During this period, the Khumbu was visited by only a few mountaineers and scientists. The expedition by Oscar and Charles Houston and Bill Tilman in 1950 had been followed in 1951 by a major Everest reconnaissance led by Eric Shipton, which nearly succeeded in passing the dreaded icefall. In 1952, the Swiss passed the icefall and almost climbed the mountain. A year later, news of the first ascent of Everest crowned Queen Elizabeth's coronation day. The mountain went untouched for another three years until the Swiss returned to make the second ascent in 1956. There were no other Everest expeditions through Nepal during the fifties, and an average of only six expeditions each year visited the entire country during the latter part of the decade.

In 1958, Colonel James O.M. "Jimmy" Roberts became the first Military Attache of the British Embassy in Kathmandu. He had joined the British Indian Army in 1936 at the age of nineteen with the intention of climbing and exploring during his annual leaves. Forbidden Nepal then held the same fascination for him that Tibet holds for today's mountaineers. After an expedition to Masherbrum in the Karakoram and many lesser climbs in other parts of India, he climbed with Tilman on Annapurna IV in 1950 with Ang Tharkay as sirdar. Roberts returned to Nepal to help with the logistics of two successful Everest expeditions, as well as to lead several other expeditions of his own. Gradually he formulated a plan for bringing adventurous tourists to the high mountains.

Now, with a firm foothold in his beloved Nepal, Roberts organized and

Above
Moonrise over Kathmandu
Upper right
Sherpa serving tea
Right
Kathmandu

led the 1960 Combined Forces expedition of British, Nepalese, and Indian officers to Annapurna II, a separate and unclimbed 26,041-foot peak about twenty-five miles from Annapurna I. Soon after, he quit the army to devote full time to mountain endeavors.

Over the years, Jimmy Roberts became thoroughly familiar with expeditionary logistics in the mountains. After serving as transportation officer to the 1963 American Everest Expedition, he decided to create his own business in Nepal, based on his high-altitude experience, his knowledge of the people and their languages, and his important friendships in the government. By a process of elimination, he narrowed the field. He did not believe in charging for his services to private mountaineering expeditions, which he saw as expressions of freedom and trust that should be kept separate from commercial involvement. He had no interest in guiding "mail-order" expeditions to lower peaks, since exposure to the dangers of mountaineering was something he believed a person should undertake on his own initiative. He saw no reason, however, why he shouldn't offer his services to tourists with adventurous spirits who would get great satisfaction from just reaching the bases of the high peaks.

In 1964 Jimmy Roberts founded Mountain Travel and registered it with the government as Nepal's first trekking agency. He took out an expensive ad in *Holiday* magazine that netted five queries, two from curious children. The business was founded well before the height of the American backpacking craze, and few people knew the meaning of "trek," a South African word used to describe a long migration by ox cart. Trekking in the Himalaya was definitely more similar to the African activity than to the American one, for packs were not carried on one's back, but by animals or men in large parties that resembled nomadic caravans.

The first Mountain Travel trek began in late February 1965, when the high mountains were too cold for climbing, but at just the time when spring would burst forth under clear skies in the valleys. The party was not quite the size that Roberts had envisioned for the 150-mile journey to Thyangboche monastery near Everest. Three women from Wisconsin and Illinois between the ages of fifty-six and sixty-four comprised this first, unprofitable, venture. Roberts had no competition in his new business for four long years.

Other events made 1965 a most decisive year for the trekking business. While the first group was in the field, the Nepalese government banned all future climbing expeditions indefinitely and closed a large area of the mountains between Annapurna and Tibet to all visitors. The official reason was national security. Mountaineering had been controversial since 1962, when four Americans applied for a peak in Nepal, then illegally crossed into Tibet for an attempt on the north side of Everest.

The more immediate cause of the closure was not revealed. In diplomatic sessions with the Nepalese, the Chinese voiced great concern over their border. Tibetan "Khamba" refugees were making a sport out of machine-gunning Chinese border guards on forays from bases in Nepal. The Chinese knew something was fishy. Normally such refugees have enough trouble feeding themselves. How could these men live at high altitude with enough leisure time to make guerilla raids with modern weapons?

The Chinese did not know the full involvement of the C.I.A. in Tibetan affairs. The agency had financed the exiled Dalai Lama's cause by flying him around the world on lecture tours and by arming and training his people. Plane loads of Khambas were secretly flown to the Mountain Warfare Training Center at Camp Hale, Colorado, beginning in 1959. They were flown back with new weapons to bases in northern Nepal from where they carried out their raids. From a secret C.I.A. airbase in Kathmandu, approximately two hundred unauthorized overflights of Tibet were made over a period of years.

The C.I.A. gradually eased out of their commitment in Tibet when it became apparent that the Khambas had little chance of winning against the Chinese occupation. The C.I.A. operation ended in 1969—the year that mountaineering in Nepal resumed.

The closure of the high peaks in 1965 had placed Sherpas in a serious economic situation. Since the Chinese had broken most of their traditional trade links with Tibet, the Sherpas had been relying on the income from an average of fourteen mountaineering expeditions a year to supplement their meager crops and grazing. The Nepalese government recognized the Sherpas' plight and endorsed trekking to fill the gap. Trekkers presumably did not have the same propensity for creating a border incident as climbers who went away from established trails to routes that were often on or close to the ill-defined border.

Another form of tourism opened in Nepal in 1965. Within sight of the high peaks were the jungles of the Tarai, an extension of the Gangetic plain of India. Here human lives were traditionally brief and unpleasant because of malaria, heat, poisonous snakes, and tigers. Only one child in three lived past infancy until the World Health Organization helped eradicate most of the malaria infestation. As they cleared the jungle to make it habitable, however, the steadily increasing population began to eradicate the Tarai's rare wildlife. After the one-horned rhinoceros became endangered, the region became first a preserve and later Royal Chitwan National Park. The park's miles of tall elephant grass formed a sanctuary for not only the last Asian rhinos, but also for Bengal tigers, leopards, sloth bears, wild boars, gaurs, monkeys, four species of deer, and nearly three hundred birds. Tributaries of the Ganges River inside the park were habitat for the highly endangered gharial crocodile and the freshwater dolphin. In November 1965 Tiger Tops Jungle Lodge opened its doors—at second-story level to accommodate visitors who traveled on the backs of elephants, from where they could experience the jungle and observe dangerous wildlife in safety. The availability of this contrasting experience made a trekking vacation in Nepal far more attractive.

The mountains of Nepal reopened for expeditions in 1969, but in a limited way. Only certain peaks were on the approved list and the north side of the Annapurna massif remained closed to everyone. The Everest area with its vistas of the world's greatest peaks set above the homeland of the Sherpas became a magnet for tourists. Roberts's little trekking business was fast becoming a phenomenon.

Mountain Travel quickly outgrew Roberts's basic four tents, eight sleeping bags, and eight place settings. Soon he had a steady stream of clients from America, England, and Australia. In 1967 he handled his first groups organized by an outside agency.

Thos. Cook and Sons—the venerable British travel firm that had sent Nepal's first tour group in 1955—now brought two trekking parties from their Oakland, California, office. Their Oakland office manager, Leo LeBon, accompanied one of the groups and talked at length with Roberts about the future of the trekking business. A year later he received Roberts's permission to form "Mountain Travel, U.S.A." LeBon's U.S. company could send adventure travel groups anywhere else in the world, but it guaranteed that its Nepal trekkers would be handled by Roberts's firm, which became known as "Mountain Travel, Nepal." LeBon had two partners: Barry Bishop and Allen Steck, both Himalayan climbers.

Scores of such firms have followed. Several travel companies and at least two publications have "adventure travel" as part of their names. And it is no wonder. Packaged adventure is in demand.

Only 8 out of the 12,567 tourists who came to Nepal in 1966 listed their purposes as trekking or mountaineering. Three years later, 293 out of 34,901 were trekkers or climbers. By 1977, seventy-two separate trekking agencies were registered to do business in Nepal, and more than a thousand travel agencies in other countries advertised treks that they booked through these Nepalese firms. A whopping 17,231 people applied for trekking permits in 1977, 4,695 of them bound for the Khumbu Valley in the newly created Sagarmatha National Park. Almost every Sherpa household had at least one person involved in the tourism business, which dominated the lifestyle of the people.

Twenty-seven years after their homeland had first been visited, the Sherpas' orientation had shifted from Tibet to the West.

Ancient trade route traversing a cliff in Nepal

The Himalaya has been described as a place where four worlds meet, and indeed at one small corner near the western end of the range China, Russia, and Afghanistan join within sight of the Pakistan border. In the eastern sector four lesser worlds meet where the narrow tip of Sikkim touches Nepal, Bhutan, and Tibet. The interminglings of language and race from these cultures seem almost infinite in possibility until yet another diversity is added: foreign travelers from the beginnings of history.

The Greeks were familiar with the Indus River civilization of India in the sixth century B.C. Armies of Alexander the Great came in the fourth century B.C., leaving in their wake a few prolific deserters from whom some modern inhabitants of Hunza, Baltistan, and Kohistan claim descent. The idea seems unlikely until one shakes hands with a blond, blue-eyed man in a crowd of his dark cousins in some remote village. Not so obvious are the genes of Genghis Khan's Mongol hordes or King Akbar's Moghul army. These and countless caravans bound to and from Central Asia account for an ethnic diversity unequalled in any other mountains. The tiny country of Nepal, for example, has at least thirty separate languages and dialects.

The photographs on the following pages are not intended to typify major groupings, but rather to give a broader picture of the mixing and intermixing of mountain peoples that continues today.

A woman and child of Manang, Nepal

Right
*Woman and child returning
from the fields,
Marsyandi River, Nepal*
Below
*Yak caravan in winter at
16,000 feet near Gokyo,
Khumbu region*

Above
*A Punjabi merchant
of Rawalpindi*
Left
*Tibetan woman
selling woolens
in Kashmir*
Below
Wash day, Kathmandu

Below
Kashmiri girl
Right
*Balti woman
in the fields
of Chongo, Karakoram*

Left
Gurung woman of Nepal
Lower left
Balti man from
Askole, Karakoram
Below
A Hunza villager with
strikingly European features

Clockwise from lower left
▶*A Sherpa boy of sixteen*
▶*A Manang trader with
partially Western clothing*
▶*Buddhist lama from Ladakh*
▶*Sunburst behind Kangtega,
Khumbu region, Nepal*

6 | Tourism and the Khumbu

Few people can cope with instant fame. The news media deluge us with sad tales of lives destroyed in the aftermath of glory. Among these celebrities are movie stars, politicians, scientists, rock singers, writers, but not mountain climbers. The reason is not that alpinists are better people, but that only two of them have become international household names, and by an accident of fortune both are men of exceptional character.

After climbing Everest in 1953, Edmund Hillary and Tenzing Norgay could have taken the easy road to riches. Instead, they turned away from the parlors of presidents and potentates and went back to the mountains. Tenzing opened a school to train Sherpas in mountaineering. Hillary began to devote several months each year to helping the Sherpa community in the Khumbu. The Himalayan Trust he helped form has built bridges, schools, and a hospital. As president of the New Zealand Volunteer Services Abroad—a sort of New Zealand peace corps—he became a watchdog of progress in Nepal's mountain areas. Instead of being merely a knighted figurehead who approved plans, and whose name brought in money, Hillary worked on Khumbu projects in the field and acted as a gadfly against economic interests that threatened the Sherpa way of life.

Hillary had strong reasons to question sudden influxes of money into the region. When, for example, a Nepalese-and-Japanese corporation sought to

Sherpa beneath Thamserku, Nepal

use the fields of Khumjung as an airstrip for the new Everest View Hotel completed in 1971, he organized an old-fashioned town meeting of the Sherpas. The company would pay money for their use of the fields and would also have a constant supply of food flown in from Kathmandu to make up for loss of production. Hillary asked the Khumjung Sherpas if they wanted "to become a dependent bunch of pensioners lining up each week for handouts of food?" They voted against the airfield and it was built a distance away from the village.

The victory did not last. The modern hotel was built near Khumjung, only twelve air miles from Mount Everest. For fifty dollars a day rich tourists could sit behind picture windows at 13,000 feet elevation and sip martinis at the bar, as isolated from the mountains as if they were seeing the Himalayas in a theater. Yet the hotel itself had a major effect on the Sherpa way of life. Airplanes coming in and going out droned into the great silence they once had. Water for cooking and cleaning had to be carried by porters from the base of the hill. The labor was done by Sherpas, and the pay contributed to the monetary inflation that had begun before the hotel was proposed. Unskilled laborers were paid ten rupees a day (eighty cents) to work on the hotel. A farm worker—drawing a plow all day—had been paid two rupees plus meals a dozen years before. Sherpas who worked on the hotel or for tourism elsewhere had to match the ten rupees to get their own fields plowed, which inflated the cost of the food they grew. By degrees, the commodities they had to buy rose to the new price level. Soon the porter or hotel laborer could buy no more with ten rupees than the field worker used to buy with two—and the field workers had been given their meals. With outside labor being brought in to work the fields while many residents worked elsewhere, the region's accustomed production of food was being distributed to more mouths. The new hotel was causing a net loss of buying power for most of the villagers, especially for those who had counted on the ten rupees a day they made from trekking as extra money, above their normal income.

To his great credit, Hillary refrained from acting as if he had every answer to the Sherpas' problems. He saw the importance of having them make their own decisions in their traditional mode. He hoped the new schools would help them make intelligent choices about their futures. He believed that the Sherpa way of life had already changed more than that of any other hill people of Nepal, but he saw the powerful role of chance in the delicate balance that was allowing them to remain in the Khumbu. Tourism had taken the place of trade, and it had come at exactly the right time. He agreed with the anthropologist Christoph von Furer-Haimendorf, who stated that "Had the Chinese stranglehold on the Sherpa's trade occurred even twenty years earlier, the effect on their standard of living would have been catastrophic . . . . A self-contained peasant economy based on agriculture and animal husbandry could not be sustained by the natural resources of valleys lying above 10,000 feet."

High altitude had helped save the Sherpa villages, since it had deterred the introduction of modern transport and technology. Sherpas lived and worked in their ancestral homes while Eskimos and other aboriginal people around the world watched reruns of Star Trek in clapboard shacks. That kind of thing was liable to happen to the Sherpas if tourism was allowed to continue without controls.

Hillary's fears were not shared by most one-time Khumbu trekkers. They saw—and still see—a paradise on earth where cheerful villagers live in the shadow of immense, inhospitable peaks. Indeed, the untrained eye had great difficulty detecting any major changes since Houston and Tilman's visit in 1950. The Sherpa people appeared as unchanged as their landscape, exhibiting the same honesty, selflessness, and cheerfulness that early Everesters had raved about. The changes to come could not be determined by the appearance of things. There was no place else in the world, however, where a wild landscape, a healthy native culture, and a heavy influx 'of tourists had coexisted for twenty-five years without grave problems.

The potential effect of tourism on the Khumbu went beyond the actions of the few thousand souls who walked into the area and up the mountain trails. In the early seventies the World Bank predicted a thirty-fold increase for tourism in Nepal before the end of the century. The attraction was Mount Everest and the Sherpa people, but most of the dollars would end up in Kathmandu. The Khumbu, like a loss leader in a chain store sale, would be sacrificed for profits elsewhere. "There is going to be terrific pressure for that money to be made," Hillary told Peter von Mertens, a Mountain Travel, U.S.A., trek leader. "And if this means that the Khumbu itself is virtually destroyed in the process, I think people will tend to be philosophical. They just see that lovely money sort of clinking into the cash register."

In the years since the first ascent of Everest, Hillary had watched the Khumbu change from a hidden sanctuary into what he called "the most surveyed, examined, blood-taken, anthropologically dissected area in the world." Yet from all the studies, there had come no report of how much change or how great a population the area could stand, and no clear plan for control of the future. Each study undertaken had to fit a succession of boxes within boxes: it had to earn the approval of the Nepalese government, correspond to the discipline of some university or agency, and provide a degree of prestige for the investigators. Hillary observed precisely what Tilman had predicted in a 1951 lecture after a visit to Nepal with a Rhodes Scholar: "Himalayan villages are not likely to reap any benefit from this enquiry, but perhaps on that account it will be more gratifying to our world planners."

A half-billion dollars in foreign aid to Nepal had done equally little to solve the dilemmas of the Khumbu. Almost every dime had gone toward the utilization, rather than preservation, of natural resources. People in high places in Nepal's government began to view the advice of rich foreigners with a jaundiced eye. The Minister of Tourism, Dr. Harka Gurung, was skeptical of experts from abroad, who "after a brief visit could consider themselves authorities on Nepalese problems."

His Royal Highness Prince Gyanendra took a personal interest in preserving the Khumbu. He listened politely to plans for potential developments, and then he conferred with the foreigners who had been in the area longest—the New Zealanders working under Hillary. At a World Wildlife Fund meeting in Bonn, Germany, in 1973, the Prince announced a bold step for his country. Sagarmatha National Park (Sagarmatha is the native name for Everest) would set aside 480 square miles of mountains and high villages as "an ecological, cultural, and geographical unit," to be managed jointly by the New Zealanders and the Nepalis. Laws governing the park were passed in 1974, but it didn't become an official preserve until July 1976. In the three years following the first announcement of the new park, the number of trekkers going to the Khumbu nearly doubled.

Overleaf
Phortse, one of the most traditional Khumbu villages

The problems were appalling. In the United States, we have trouble enough trying to deal with the basic conflict between preservation and public use. After five years of highly emotional public hearings we have yet to agree on a master plan for Yosemite. Picture, however, a Yosemite or Yellowstone park with people living in it, a fragile native culture to be protected intact. To the simple duties of management, add the requirements of agriculture, social change, deforestation, local inflation, and energy use. All this and much more confronted Gordon Nichols, the New Zealand Project Manager in charge of the park.

Even if all the individual quandaries were solvable, creation of the park had one inescapable effect on the Sherpa culture: The parklands were under public control; there was no way to get around this. No matter how many responsibilities were given back to the Sherpas, they knew in their hearts that they had become wards in their homeland. The Sherpas' traditional ways had been deeply rooted in absolute home rule of their villages and lives.

Before tourism came, Sherpa societies had a noticeable absence of internal strife. A person's position in his village was the center of his life. Every action was judged by how it affected the community, which resolved conflicts by discussion. All except the most recent Khamba immigrants were members of what we would label the middle class. Enough of life was dependent on subsistence agriculture to make each individual responsible for a great deal of manual labor. Yet enough trading took place to allow a degree of upward mobility. The rich never became too rich, because customary Sherpa generosity led anyone who received a windfall profit to share it with the community. Parties, ritual celebrations, and the construction of chortens and mani walls were commonly financed by individuals.

The economics of tourism made it less necessary for a Sherpa to maintain allegiance to his community. Many men now lived away from their homes for long periods of time. Only because tradition was so strong would these people follow the old customs when they returned. The creation of the national park strained the old allegiances even more. The trekking Sherpa is now confronted by a moral choice between the approval of his community, the laws governing the national park, and his livelihood.

This new triangle of morality showed immediate effects during the year Sagarmatha National Park was created. The Sherpas' energy crisis—already severe—worsened immediately after strict public regulations against woodcutting were introduced.

Before tourists and expeditions started coming to the Khumbu, the slow-growing forests near high villages were carefully protected. Green wood was never cut, and each village appointed forest guards to watch over the local communal forest, in which cutting was not allowed. Wood needs for outsiders were minimal. A traveling trader might build an occasional cooking fire; a visiting family might temporarily increase a household's needs. But when the expeditions started coming, vast amounts of wood were cut, and the cutting was done by Sherpas who were away from their home villages.

Although there is no precise record of the early condition of the Khumbu, Hillary had an experience that made him realize suddenly the changes he had seen in small increments over the years. In 1976 he made a journey into a side valley in the Khumbu region where few, if any, trekkers had traveled. From a high pass he dropped below 13,000 feet into a thick forest of rhododendron—

not the flower we know in America, but the same plant nurtured by monsoons into fifty-foot trees that make superb firewood. Farther down the valley he entered a healthy pine forest surrounded by almost impenetrable juniper. After he had returned, he told Peter von Mertens about his experience.

"It really did bring back to me, 'My God this was how the Khumbu was when we first went in there.' You turned the corner at Pheriche and the whole place was a deep green, clothed in juniper right up the valley and up beside the glacier everywhere. Well, of course, now you have to look pretty hard to even see a single bush anywhere.

"We were the ones who started cutting it out, I might say. In the Everest reconnaissance in 1951 we carried it up to the Khumbu Glacier. And in 1952 the Swiss cut 400 porter loads of the juniper—so much that when we went back in 1953 on our successful climb, there were still about 100 loads of the Swiss stuff all stacked up on the ice, which we were able to use. We also went to work and hacked up a couple hundred more loads just locally. Now the juniper has virtually been wiped out. The whole area up there is just a desert now which is all eroding."

In 1963 Nepal democratized the entire nation by dividing it into a series of local governments called *panchayats*. Forests that were not on privately owned land became state forests, controlled by the district *panchayat* rather than by the community's forest guards, who became obsolete once their authority was taken away. Permits for felling enough timber to build a house had to come from the district office, which in the Khumbu was four days' walk from the main villages. Few bothered with this red tape, and since no forest department officials were stationed in the Khumbu, unauthorized cutting became rampant. Hillsides near major villages were denuded as the pressure for firewood kept increasing. The Khumbu's population doubled between 1950 and 1970 both from an influx of Tibetan refugees and from the results of modern medical care. Many Sherpas on treks had to hire Tamang people from lower villages to work their fields, creating more need for firewood. And with each trek or expedition came a swarm of foreigners who wanted local wood. Then came the national park.

A law was passed allowing Sherpas to continue burning wood in the park, but forcing trekkers to use kerosene. However kerosene was not readily available so the law was temporarily lifted. The Sherpas watched in awe as the national park set up shop by cutting incredible amounts of timber for their building needs. Hillary commented, "They have been chopping down more trees and sawing up more timber than anybody else. The local people, although they have been assured they will still have access to timber and firewood, don't believe it. They think that once the national park and the big wheelers and dealers have got all their wood, there will be a clamp-down on the availability of timber. And so the Sherpas have been also cutting timber—laying in a stock. There is virtually no house in the whole of Khumbu that doesn't have a good reserve supply of timber."

The Sherpas were no longer placing the good of their village as the highest priority; it was every man for himself. When a trekking group or expedition bought wood—by weight—they were often sold heavy green wood, in direct conflict with old village rules designed to protect young trees.

Kerosene may never be an economically feasible cooking fuel for the Sherpas. It must either be flown in at great expense or carried sixteen days from

Left
Construction work in Namche Bazaar,
Khumbu region, Nepal
Lower Left
Trekkers in the Khumbu region below Ama Dablam
Lower right
Sherpa girl gathering green firewood, Khumbu

the Indian border. In 1978, the price in the Khumbu was $2.50 a gallon. That's almost two days' pay to a Sherpa, the equivalent of $100-per-gallon kerosene in the United States.

Austrian foreign aid is funding a small hydroelectric plant, due to be completed by 1981. Located near Namche Bazaar, it will provide an initial 260,000 watts of power to the villages of Khumjung and Kunde as well. Cost-conscious Nepali civil engineers who designed the project estimated that underground power lines would be eleven times more expensive than conventional ones. For ease of maintenance in winter, overhead lines will parallel the Mount Everest trail. And on a chill autumn evening not too far in the future, a group of trekkers may have the choice of watching alpenglow on Everest or Star Trek.

Energy use in the Khumbu has far more parameters than firewood, kerosene, or electricity. David Brower, president of Friends of the Earth, co-led a trekking group in the Khumbu with Peter von Mertens in 1976. Beyond the seriousness of the wood crisis, he saw some things to be thankful for. Agriculture was basically unchanged. No foreign experts had been there to increase the yield per acre.

One night he told his group, "I have an admiration that has known no bounds so far when I compare what they've done with their agriculture for so long, with what we've done with ours so recently. We will have to learn from other countries how to make agriculture work without pouring so much oil into the ground, figuratively, which is what we've done. The overall U.S. average is that it takes ten times as much energy to get food to your mouth as you will get out of it, calorie for calorie. A lot of fertilizing, motorized equipment, processing, transportation, refrigeration, and cooking. In the U.S. in wet rice agriculture we put five times as much energy into growing the rice as we get out of the rice when we eat it. In Southeast Asia they get fifty times as much energy *out* as they put in; here in Nepal the ratio is probably around twenty-five times as much out of the rice as they put into it.

"When we go to help people we give them some tool the consequences of which we haven't contemplated. Take that simple wooden plow we've seen—not behind two buffalo, but just a long stick, nicely crafted, not too fancy, and very easy to carry. The beauty of it is that you can lift it from terrace to terrace. The United States started to help some of the poor benighted hill-farmers [at lower elevations] by giving them modern, heavy plows that could not be lifted terrace to terrace. The farmers had to make ramps, and they got new erosion channels . . . . "

When monsoon rains hit the notched terraces, more precious topsoil was inadvertently exported to the island in the Bay of Bengal. The fields, if they didn't slide into rivers, became less productive than before.

This process has yet to happen in the Khumbu, but there is one indication that it could. Plowing has traditionally been done by teams of three or four Sherpas. With the recent shortage of labor in the villages during the trekking season, almost all plowing is now done with heavy yak-oxen crossbreeds (dzos) that can pull far larger equipment than has previously been used.

The steady increase in grazing animals has had another important effect on the land. When the Sherpas realized that their forests were in danger, they attempted reforestation themselves. Their saplings didn't survive the first season, because yaks trampled or uprooted them. The national park is sur-rounding plots of their new 800-acre reforestation project with stone fences. However, a healthy yak fueled by monsoon vegetation is a formidable creature that doesn't hesitate to walk through a wall if the grass is greener on the other side.

Another park project is the restoration and maintenance of religious monuments and buildings, a duty formerly assumed by the Sherpas. Their lack of recent attention underscores their movement away from traditional, community-focused life. The anthropologist Von Furer-Haimendorf noted many changes between his visits to the Khumbu in 1957 and 1971. Not one Buddhist inscription had been added to the chorten and mani walls of Khum-jung and Kunde; previously, new work was always being done. The number of lamas in Thyangboche monastery had dropped from thirty-two to fourteen. Two lamas had hired on as porters for an expedition without even informing the abbot. Before tourism and the Hillary schools, the monasteries offered the only opportunity to learn reading and writing. Now, education is funded partly by tourism. Earnings from tourism are also being invested in the creation of new tourist facilities in the villages. The lamas who are left tell those who will listen that they feel quite a conflict between constantly having to deal with tourists and the more important business of living an exemplary religious life.

When the first adventurers traveled the Khumbu, they stayed as guests in Sherpa homes for no charge. When trekkers began paying for the privilege, some Sherpas built tea houses or additions specifically as tourist quarters. The government, however, is assisting the building of lodges and small hotels by

Right
Firewood at Lukla, Khumbu region
Below
*Sherpas carrying firewood
to the Everest View Hotel
at 12,500 feet.*

outside interests. Companies in Kathmandu can receive loans through the Nepal Industrial Development Corporation for building in the Khumbu. A few trekkers' lodges already exist, and more are planned.

This development is only possible because of the exclusion of large areas of land from the national park. Hillary, who helped found the park, thought it would include the entire Khumbu Valley. He was as surprised as anyone when he discovered "all the grazing areas and every area where there is going to be anybody building a tea house or a junk shop or possible hotel are excluded. As far as I can detect, not one of the national park buildings that is being constructed is actually on park land."

The scenario for Khumbu trekking in the future is one of a series of hotels and lodges all the way to Everest Base Camp. There will be one Sherpa for each twenty-five trekkers, a considerable departure from the four or five that are now employed for each group of about a dozen trekkers who camp en route. Fewer Sherpas will guide in their homeland; more will go far afield. An official in His Majesty's Tourism Department has even voiced the idea of moving all the Sherpas out of the Khumbu, but such a forced exodus is highly unlikely. Tomorrow's trekkers will need to do nothing but place one foot in front of the other; the lodge system will do the rest. Reaching the base of Everest will require little more self-direction than checking into a Holiday Inn. The traditional unknowns of early expeditions—organizing, budgeting, routefinding, hiring, bargaining, communicating, buying food, finding shelter, deciding where to drink and where to defecate—will all be decided in advance. The greatest loss will be a psychological one. Their visit to the Everest region, unlike Hillary's, will not force them to see that parts of the world are better off without Western values.

Experts in resource management, anthropology, and economics often state that the Sherpa people should be allowed to choose, and are already choosing, their own course toward Westernization. According to this reasoning, Sherpa eyes turned from East to West at the simultaneous closing of Tibet and opening of Nepal. We should expect these seminomadic traders to seek increasing contacts with the modern world now that Thyangboche Monastery is closer in travel time to New York than it once was to Lhasa, and now that the arrival of tourists is as predictable as that of the monsoon.

To accept the extinction of the old Sherpa way of life as a foregone conclusion is as inexcusable as accepting the extinction of species as a natural course beyond our control. At stake is the long-range continuity of the world into which we were born and a set of conditions that allow human existence on this planet in spite of cosmic improbability. The key question is how these high-sounding ideals mesh with the choices available in the Khumbu.

Before we seek the answers, we must recognize the basic difference between the new trade in tourism and the old in commodities. The Sherpa community once had direct control over the flow of salt, wool, and grain, and it strengthened the Sherpas' bonds with each other. Today's flow of tourists, who book Everest Base Camp with their travel agent and enter a national park controlled by the government, weakens the community bonds. There are ways to strengthen the society and renew the old ties. New jobs in the Khumbu should be a primary concern. As mountaineering becomes ever more popular, guiding for climbs on the lower peaks could be arranged directly in the high villages (as in Chamonix or Jackson Hole) instead of with agencies outside the district; the present system operates within regulations designed for the ascent of Everest rather than that of a day-climb. As education and medicine continue to make inroads into the Khumbu, Sherpas can be trained to work in these capacities in their homes. Arts and crafts, now chiefly involved with selling refugees' belongings as "Very Old Tibetan" artifacts, could be reoriented into an industry based on present, traditional skills. An energy source that provides an alternative to the proposed overhead power lines from small hydroelectric plants is simply the sun. Solar energy has limitations in its present technology, but it could greatly reduce dependence on wood in a place where the people are not yet addicted to a constant supply of instant power and heat. Only foreign capital could bring about this switch.

The exodus of Sherpas into the business world of Kathmandu is often cited as an example of the coming Westernization, but these emigrants tend to come from the fringes of Khumbu society, rather than from the core of old clans. When trekking and climbing were first introduced, members of poor families and landless refugees from Tibet were the most likely to take the risks inherent in hiring on with outsiders. To a great extent the old families missed out on these early fruits of the tourist boom, but their continued presence in the Khumbu today, after the most daring entrepreneurs and opportunists have left for the lowlands or died on the heights, insures a core of stability and old traditions that gives them a fighting chance to beat the odds that are working against every population of mountain dwellers on earth.

7

Around Annapurna

While our guided expedition was on Nun Kun, the Manang District in Nepal near the Tibetan border suddenly opened after twelve years of closure. My lady Jo Sanders arranged our trip, including a Sherpa crew and many of the services given a standard trek. Our personal gear would be carried, our camp would be set up each day, and our meals would be served in a mess tent. We asked Kim to join us.

We looked forward to making the 200-mile circle of the Annapurna massif in the footsteps of Tilman's and Herzog's 1950 expeditions. The itinerary offered a great contrast to trekking in the Khumbu, since it didn't double back on itself and it traversed a more expansive cross-section of culture and geography. We would start in a monsoon-drenched jungle at 1,400 feet and reach 17,700 feet in an arid Tibetan moonscape before descending into the deepest canyon in the world. The basic trip would be walking, but we planned to carry one rope, crampons, and ice axes. We would travel up the long Marsyandi Valley, which had been closed to trekking, and end in the canyon of the Kali Gandaki, where tourists and even an airstrip had exposed the residents to the outside world for many years.

With the trip plans confirmed, we decided to invite a few more friends. Jo invited an easy-going couple from Berkeley, Ray Juncosa and Liz Gibson, engineer and accountant, respectively. Ray was a very fit long-distance runner who had been to the Khumbu before. Our trip would give him the opportunity

The fairytale village of Braga

to share his excitement for Nepal with his fiancée. I invited Vern Clevenger and Virginia Parker. Vern was a 21-year-old bundle of energy and rock climbing talent who had taken Yosemite and the High Sierra by storm. His speed and skill were legendary, but so was his ability to inadvertently destroy equipment. In California mountain jargon, the verb "to clevenger" meant to break prematurely, as in zippers, skis, tents, cars, and toilet seats. Virginia was a full-blooded Indian born in Yosemite. Neither of them had traveled outside of North America. My third guest was also a first-time traveler. Gerry Gregg had raced hot rods with me as a youth. Later, we used to solve the world's problems once a week over lunch while he was a political science professor and I owned a small automotive business. We still had much in common, because we both had given up those careers to devote more time to the wilderness. Gerry loved twenty-mile days in the Sierra, and I was sure he would be captivated by Nepal.

The tone of the trip, however, was to be set by Kim's single invitee. Carl Gustafson was a civil engineer in his mid-forties who lived near Lake Tahoe, California. His *curriculum vitae* was typical for a Himalayan trekker: high income, good education, and good physical condition. He was a generous man, but not the sort that joins a service club. Carl had an entirely different manner of showing loyalty to his fellow beings. Sometimes the lot of a person he had known ten minutes would lead him to crush a wad of bills into his palm or give him the shirt off his back. But the plight of someone wronged by authority turned this six-foot-four burly Swede into a one-man army. Alcohol enhanced Carl's ability to discover the wrongs of society; he had been permanently expelled from nearly every bar within a fifty-mile radius of his home. This was a considerable feat, since that circle included not only the little towns of Truckee and Tahoe City, but also the countless casinos of Stateline and Reno.

Once, when Carl saw a policeman strike a woman friend, he charged into the fracas and was beaten and handcuffed by assisting officers. As soon as he was allowed to stand (with his hands locked behind his back), he lunged at the officer who had hit the woman and bit him in the crotch, not letting go until he lost consciousness from the drumbeat of flashlights upon his skull.

Carl had trekked across the glaciers of the remote Hongu region of Nepal, and had gotten on famously with the Sherpas. Their tolerance and code of honor appealed to him, and he was anxious to repeat that experience. The Manangbhots, however, were reputed to be the most fierce and inhospitable people in Nepal.

The ease of our passage across the very crest of the Himalaya was made possible by a quirk in Himalayan geography. Some of the rivers predate the uplift of the exceptionally young range. As the land rose, their waters cut gorges across the crest, unlike those of American rivers that remained confined on one side or the other of the Continental Divide.

Our route around the Annapurna massif would follow the Marsyandi River past where it had cut a 21,000-foot-deep gorge through the Himalayan crest into Manang—geographically on the Tibetan side but politically in Nepal. From there a trail would take us over a 17,700-foot pass into the Kali Gandaki, the world's deepest canyon. The walls of the canyon rise 23,000 feet to the peaks of Annapurna and Dhaulagiri. Eventually we would complete a 250-mile orbit of Annapurna—all on trails that had been used by Himalayan traders for a thousand years.

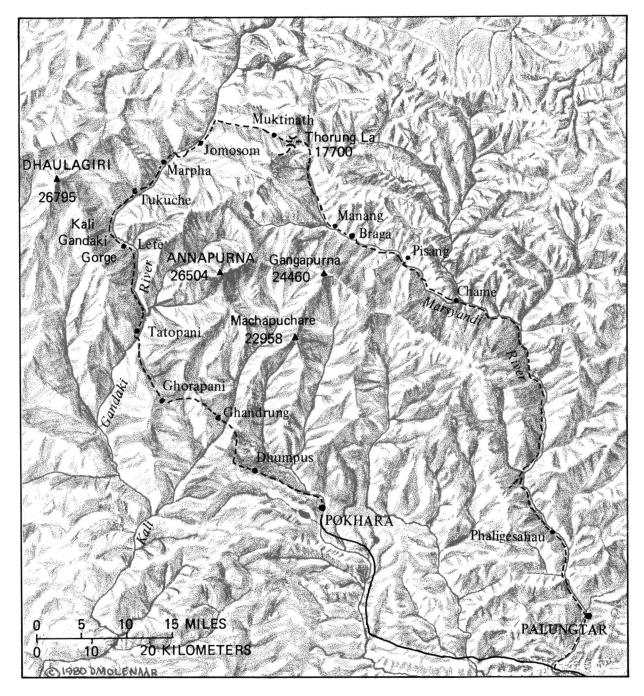

Route around
Annapurna

The first-timers were awed by the humid and pungent air of India that seemed as if it could be cut with a knife. Kathmandu, on the other hand, provided a pleasant surprise; we stepped off the airplane into a cool, clear world, surrounded by snowy peaks set into a moonlit sky.

The efficiency of mountain tourism in Nepal can equal the best to be found in America. After only one day in Kathmandu, all our preparations and formalities were complete. At 6:00 A.M. on November 1, Land Rovers picked us up for a four-hour drive to the trailhead. We watched the land come alive as we followed rolling hills on a narrow, paved highway that had been built by the Chinese. Sunlight turned terraced fields iridescent green against a backdrop of rising mist and blue sky. People flowed out of thatch-roofed houses and along narrow trails toward the work of the day. The trucks dropped us at the trailhead, and our gear was distributed to porters and packed into loads. In just half an hour the porters were on the trail, and our young Sherpa sirdar, Tsering Ongchu, was motioning us to go.

At only 1,400 feet the beginning of the trek was far hotter than it had been in Kathmandu. Even though it was November, the temperatures were in the eighties and the air was moist. We walked in shorts and running shoes through fields of rice, millet, beans, and mustard while the summit of Himalchuli hung cloudlike above us in the haze. We were served a leisurely lunch under a giant banyan tree while the porters marched on ahead. By the time we reached camp in the afternoon, everything was waiting for us. Vern, who was used to living in the High Sierra for weeks on almost nothing, couldn't believe what he saw. "It fulfills the dreams of all those hot days in the mountains when I've rounded a corner and hoped to see what I saw today: camp all set up with tea and cookies waiting on a table."

As the trail started to climb out of the plains, the population became increasingly Buddhist. Thatched huts disappeared, and at the village of Bagarchap we saw our first gompa set on a hill above stone houses. Jo and I were invited into a Buddhist home where we were served rice beer, *chang*. Camp that day was at Temung Meadows, at 8,500 feet on a hill above the river. At dark, a thick cloud of mist flowing up the canyon began to rise toward us. We looked out over a continuous blanket of white broken only by the ramparts of Manaslu glowing far above the clouds in the last light. The mist engulfed us. The contours of the rugged landscape were softened, and all sounds were muted.

Early the next morning we passed a French trekking group going in the opposite direction. Our hellos were met with hostile stares, an increasingly common occurrence along heavily traveled Himalayan trails.

Travelers in remote areas have always welcomed each other and had meals together. Some modern trekkers, however, suffer from a peculiar xenophobia. The exceptions to tradition are not friends traveling together, but individuals being guided on a commercial adventure, who have little feeling of remoteness as they move along with an umbilical cord attached to a Sherpa army. They avoid contacts that might remind them that they have paid someone else to deal with the hazards and unknowns. In letters home and in articles for hometown papers, they omit references to companies or guides that would give away the fact that they are not involved in the day-to-day decisions of their journey. And along the trail they feel uncomfortable making small talk to others who might be doing the same thing.

At the tail end of the French party was a heartwarming surprise—the

broadly smiling face of Ang Tsering, the Sherpa who had been with us on Nun Kun. Here, seven months after we had climbed together in Ladakh, we were meeting by chance in Nepal. We opened our arms and hugged each other, and after a brief moment with expressions of joy, he rushed off to catch his charges.

Our day's travel ended in a pine glade at Chame, a check point for entry into the Manang District. Beyond Chame we experienced the most amazing geographical change of the journey as we walked the few miles to Pisang. The heavy luxurious forest so typical of middle altitudes in Nepal suddenly disappeared as we turned a great right-angle corner in the river valley. Lush pines and firs were replaced by scraggly junipers, sagebrush, and bare earth. If we had climbed up and down over the crest of the range the shift in life zones would not have seemed so abrupt. But we had crossed the crest of the mountain range on the floor of a deep valley.

The great corner itself was an amphitheater of granitic rock as consistently smooth as a sandy beach. Slabs rose unbroken out of grasslands for at least 4,000 feet to the crest of a ridge. Each afternoon, masses of cloud from the lowlands rode the winds up the river valley, arriving at the great corner aimed gently upward. When the plume hit the curving planes of rock, it turned ninety degrees before diffusing into the clear Tibetan sky.

As I wrote down the description in my diary, I realized that I had made the basic assumption that the wind was guided by the shape of the valley. What, I wondered, if the daily cloud plume had made the great corner instead of the other way around? During the monsoon, the plume would build each day, hit the cliff, and dissipate into the sky. When I thought of how timberline trees had been sculpted into rounded forms by mere hundreds of years of far less consistent forces, I wondered about the power of a massive Himalayan air current spread over eons of time and a few thousand feet of rock. There may well be a better explanation for the sudden appearance of the outsized, smooth slabs that we saw nowhere else in the region, but mine, for the moment, answered my question of why such an unusual formation occurred at precisely the spot where the moist air of the lower Marsyandi passed onto the Tibetan plateau.

Each of us shared the impression that we were somewhere in the Great Basin of North America—like Tibet, a high continental plain in the rain shadow of lofty mountains. The traffic, however, was considerably different from that on Interstate 80. Yak trains bearing firewood passed us several times a day. The caravans were reminiscent of the days when Manang was a trade route for wool, silver, salt, and furs from Central Asia that were exchanged for grain, iron, cotton, and cattle from Nepal.

The local people didn't know what to make of Virginia, the first American Indian to visit the area. They looked askance when we tried to explain what an "Indian" was. It was interesting to me that the yak men of Manang had features, clothing, and hair styles that bore an uncanny resemblance to those of the Plains Indians from America. The similarity of the landscape only heightened the comparison.

Since our Sherpas had no love for the Manangbhots, we camped two miles short of the town in fields next to the Marsyandi River. Above us was another village, Braga, set into a cliff like an illustration in a fairytale. Tiers of rock houses rose upward until they culminated in the final building—a white gompa fronted by a great brass bell. A snowy mountain peeked over the top of the cliff, adding a sense of wholeness to a scene that seemed to represent all the elements of the land in just the right proportions.

Our planned itinerary called for two days of rest and acclimatization at Braga before heading up the 17,700-foot Thorung La. We were apprehensive about visiting the nearby village of Manang, both because of the villagers' fierce reputation and because of Carl's predictable reaction toward those who take too much power for themselves. On the first afternoon, Carl and Kim decided to visit Manang, and they asked if anyone else wanted to go. I was the only taker. As the three of us walked toward what appeared to be a stone fortress in the distance, I felt as if I was heading for Idi Amin's stronghold with a Hell's Angel.

To the south of the village a great icefall dropped from Gangapurna into a green, glacial lake. The town itself had no such variety of beauty. All we could see was stone. Each house was a multistory stone edifice. The millions of stones within eyesight overpowered our senses. We did not see the piles of wood or hay, the wooden ladders, or the prayer flags, but only a world of stone. Walking down alleyways where we could touch both walls, we felt a sense of cold claustrophobia as if we were in a prison cellblock. There was little sign of activity and the place seemed like a ghost town. When we did see faces, they were as hard as the stone itself. Our gazes were met with arrogant stares. We understood why Maurice Herzog had left Manang almost empty-handed after trying to buy provisions for his Annapurna porters in 1950. We found no place to stop and relax—no tea house, no bazaar, nothing but dungeons of stone as far as we could see.

At the far end of town a harsh voice yelled down from a balcony: "Hey, you! You wanna buy a rug? Twenty-thousand rupees!" The accent was that of an American street hood.

Kim looked up at a young Manangbhot who was dusting a Tibetan carpet. Their eyes met and Kim yelled back, "One thousand rupees; no more!"

"You come up here!" the Manangbhot answered. We climbed a ladder hewn out of pine log and faced five Manangbhots on the balcony of a large stone house. All were dressed in a blend of homespun woolens and Western clothing that didn't clash in appearance because denim, wool, and skin alike were gilded by the dust of the village. Several of the men showed complete indifference to us, while the others made it clear that they were only interested in our wallets. When they pushed Carl into naming a price for their rug, he said eight hundred rupees—lowering Kim's bid and offering a mild insult that brought a look of instant respect. Only then—half an hour after we had come up to the balcony—were we invited into the house.

The large single room was almost totally dark at midday. There were no windows. Above the fire in the hearth was a hole in the ceiling that brought in a spotlight of sun and let out some of the smoke. The smoke billowed by our faces toward the soot-filled shelves and corners. Here in this primitive dwelling with no chimney and no hint of the discovery of the wheel was a Thai Airlines calendar with a photo of a Boeing 747.

Our hosts led a dual existence. In Manang they followed traditional ways—growing crops, marrying local women, and living in simplicity. In the winter, however, they traveled by jet to such places as Bangkok, Singapore, and Tokyo where they traded Tibetan carpets and artifacts for gems, gold, and silk that they could exchange for grain, cattle, tea, and tobacco in Nepal. Most

Upper left
Inside a Nepali home, Tal, Marsyandi River
Left
Woman of the fields, Upper Marsyandi River
Above
Great Buddha of the Braga gompa
Right
Waterfall in Marsyandi Gorge

of the men had already left for the season. The 747 on the wall was as much a part of these legendary traders' lives as the primitive village we were now seeing. When two wives came in with young children, I was amazed at how pleasant and modest they were in comparison to their arrogant, defiant husbands. Far from being submissive, however, these women were fully in control of their world. Each had more than one husband, and they frequently traveled on their own to other parts of Nepal to barter for food and grain while their men were in more distant places. They ran the village for at least half the year.

Although we were served *rakshi* (rice whisky) in wooden cups, it was clear that this was not so much a welcome as a greasing of the wheels of commerce. The Manangbhots had the kind of life that many Westerners dream about: spending one half of the year in a profession that allows them to travel to exotic places, and the other half in a remote mountain fastness with their families. We represented the intrusion of the wrong half at the wrong time.

We walked back to camp emptyhanded with our wallets intact, planning to go elsewhere tomorrow rather than meet another cold reception in Manang. At dinner, Jo's eyes lit up as she told me how different her experience in Braga had been. The people were kind and open. She had spent a wonderful hour alone on a rooftop balcony with a woman who was nearly a hundred years old. Unlike the square fortification of Manang, the village of Braga had a natural openness because of its position on the cliffside. Buildings were made of stone, yet one's whole horizon wasn't pervaded by stone. The ice-laden Annapurna massif was always in sight, a running wall forty miles long and from 24,000 to 26,500 feet high. The river valley and the forests gave a feeling of closeness with nature that was totally lacking in Manang.

Despite our group's diversity, the nine of us got on well together. We had some mixtures that could have been dynamite in other situations, but they stayed defused because everyone was tolerant of each other's individualism. The three couples formed the core, with Kim and Carl an independent and separate force. The odd man, Gerry, managed to be friends with all and foe to none.

The next morning Jo wanted to take me up through the village of Braga to revisit the people and the ancient gompa she had discovered the day before. Kim, Carl, Vern, and Virginia headed off toward the great ice lake of Tilicho before dawn for a long day-hike. At over 16,000 feet, this three-mile-long frozen lake was one of the highest bodies of water of its size in the world. In the icy northern shadow of the high peaks, it was in a totally uninhabited area far off normal trade or trekking routes.

When Jo and I set off for Braga, Gerry and Ray decided to join us. We wound up through the village toward the holy gompa nestled in the hillside high above the last house. A lama opened the front doors to expose a kneeling buddha that filled a multistory hall. I asked if I could take a photograph from far to the side where a support post rose from floor to ceiling. As I looked through the viewfinder I was reminded of another shrine in my own country, where I had felt great awe in the presence of a single statue in an expansive room. In my imagination the tall wooden post became concrete; the statue in robes lost its Asian eyefolds and gained a beard; the lama watching my every move became a National Park policeman. I didn't tell the others that I saw something of the Lincoln Memorial in the Braga gompa, because it might have sounded disrespectful at the time. However, the more I learned about the area, the more the similarity held true. The gompa had gradually been evolving into a historical landmark, rather than the center of the villager's world. There are fewer lamas than before, and most all the scrolls, *thankas* and thousand-odd small silver buddhas are coated with a thick layer of dust. The Nepali anthropologist Dor Bahadur Bista writes that the people "are nominally Buddhist, but give little thought or care to religion and have allowed their few temples and monasteries to fall into general disrepair." An influx of Tibetan refugees during the fifties and sixties caused some revitalization of old traditions, but probably not enough to stem the tide of increasing outside influences—especially tourism.

Long after darkness fell and we had finished dinner, the Tilicho foursome returned. They had been unable to get anywhere near the remote lake. A rocky hill that had appeared to be only a couple of hours' walk away in the clear mountain air was still above them after they had walked hard into the afternoon. Carl's feet were blistered and he had fallen into an icy stream, but he glowingly told of seeing snow leopard tracks crossing the trail. Carl had a strong interest in and knowledge of wildlife, and this evidence of the passage of such an elusive creature was just the kind of thing he had come to Nepal to experience.

All of us were looking forward to the next few days, when we would rise above habitation into a zone of the Himalaya that appeared unchanged by humanity. We would move from 11,000 to nearly 18,000 feet in two days. If the weather was clear on the pass, Kim, Vern, and I planned to camp there and make a day climb for some unusual views of Annapurna I, a peak that was hidden from all northern vantage points on our trekking route. Like Herzog in 1950, we longed to see for ourselves what was behind the "Great Barrier" of lower peaks that blocked access to Annapurna.

8 | The Beavers of Muktinath

Joseph Dalton Hooker spent three years in the Himalaya studying natural history. His primary interest was botany. In eastern Nepal he observed how plants had adapted themselves to special conditions of the environment; he saw that wildlife, too, fit this pattern. He extended this conclusion to include human residents, remarking how an ethnic "change in the population accompanies that in the natural features of the country."

Today, Hooker's manner of thinking is commonplace, but it was revolutionary at the time of his travels. He went to Nepal in 1847, a dozen years before the publication of Darwin's theory of evolution. His work became recognized as the botanical basis of Darwinian thought, and he was knighted by the Queen.

The Himalaya after Hooker, like the Galápagos after Darwin, took on a special prominence in scientific circles. Botanists and zoologists joined mountaineering expeditions to bring back rare specimens for museums and universities abroad, but the studies of ecology and behavior that Hooker initiated came to a virtual standstill.

In 1950, the Himalaya was one of the least-studied regions of the world. No one had followed up on Hooker's observation that Himalayan people, like plants and lower animals, were limited by the habitat available to them.

The exotic culture of Nepalese hill people disguises an underlying dependence on the constancy of local conditions. Their plight is strikingly similar to

Hindu temple of Jiwala Mayi, Muktinath

that of animals who have the ability to make major changes in their own habitat. Wood poses the major resource problem for today's mountain people, just as it does for the beaver, whose colonies thrive only so long as a source is close at hand. When beavers must travel a long distance for wood, their ability to feed, breed, and protect their young declines. Without wood, the colony disappears.

The worst wood problems in Nepalese villages are yet to come, but Muktinath in the Manang District north of Annapurna provides a sneak preview; long the destination of Hindu and Buddhist pilgrims, it has had more than normal population pressure for centuries.

The goal of the pilgrims is not a temple of one religion, but a mystical power from the earth itself that draws Hindus, Buddhists, and ancient Bon-Pos alike. All these religions recognize that there is a vital force at the confluence of rivers. The gateway to Muktinath is in the Kali Gandaki Gorge at the junction of the Jhong Khola and the Thak Khola rivers. The holy place is high above the confluence on the eastern slope of the gorge, where the powers of earth, fire, and water miraculously come together. The pilgrim peers into a crack in the rocks where a flame burns on the surface of flowing water, the result of natural gas escaping beneath a stream bed. Next to the stream in a grove of cottonwoods is a Hindu temple of the flame goddess, Jiwala Mayi, a reincarnation of the great god Vishnu. For Hindus, the shrine holds the power of *Mukti*, which will deliver them from the sufferings of their mortal life into an infinite spiritual existence. They annoint themselves in 108 fountains that carry the sacred waters. Tibetan Buddhists share the same deity, calling her Chumik Gyasa, and they have built a small gompa over the source of the flame. Muktinath has special significance for them because it lies above the path by which the seeds of Buddhism were brought to Tibet from Nepal over 1200 years ago: the Kali Gandaki.

From a distance Muktinath appears to be an oasis in the middle of a desert. Its green fields and groves of cottonwoods contrast with a brown landscape totally devoid of trees. To the traveler, this image adds to the mystical appeal of the place, but it has not always been this way, and the change has not been purposeful. The village now suffers from a shortage of wood, which—unlike that in the Khumbu—was already serious before the tourists came. A century ago, cottonwoods lined the stream both above and below the village. Willows thrived in their shade. Great forests of birch clung to north-facing slopes not far from town. The residents of Muktinath harvested these trees to burn for heat and cooking, to build their homes and shrines, and to use as fodder for their livestock. Only a sacred forest in the immediate vicinity of the shrines was left standing.

Each household in Muktinath burns an average of seventeen pounds of wood each day, more than six thousand pounds each year. One man who was born in a forest a mile from the shrine still lives in his ancestral home, but it is now surrounded by desert. Winds have removed the last vestige of topsoil and only a few scraggly plants of the sage community manage to survive. Even the scrub hemlock on higher slopes is rapidly being depleted for fuel, since the nearest forest (a mere remnant of green growth near the upper Jhong Khola River) is now two hours of uphill walking away. A larger, but more heavily cut, forest lies in the Panda Khola Valley on the opposite side of the Kali Gandaki Gorge, even farther away. There, birch, fir, and rhododendron grow on steep northern exposures., a hard three-hour walk from Muktinath. The biggest, most accessible trees have been felled; many lie on the shoals of the river, waiting to be cut up and transported to the village. Because of the distance involved, human portage is being replaced by packtrains of mules or dzos that forage daily on the barren hills.

Stockpiles of wood on the roofs and balconies of Muktinath dwellings are no larger or smaller than in the past, but an increasing portion of each villager's year is devoted to gathering or paying for it. Now there is little free time or extra money to maintain the holy shrines. The gompa has become decrepit. Its artwork has faded and peeled; the curtain that protects the eternal flame is as ragged as beggars' clothing. Even the guest house for pilgrims has become barely habitable.

The people of Muktinath became aware of their wood crisis twenty years ago. They began to plant seedlings by the river and alongside irrigation canals. Many of the seedlings were eaten or trampled by the increasing herds of livestock, but others grew into a source that is just now being used. Although the reforestation provided not nearly enough wood for the villagers' normal needs, it was a start toward minimizing the most time-consuming chore of their lives.

Then came tourism.

Muktinath opened to trekkers late in 1976. It had been open a few times in the past, but only a handful of foreigners had come to this dead end in the heart of Khumbu country. Early in 1977, the opening of Manang District put Muktinath on the itinerary of every trekker making the orbital walk around Annapurna, which instantly became second only to Everest Base Camp as the most popular long trek in the Himalaya. By 1978, more than 3,500 tourists had visited Muktinath and most of them camped for the night. Nearly all imagined that they were helping the native economy by paying three dollars for a load of firewood.

Muktinath's wood problems are not yet shared by the village of Manang on the opposite side of the 17,700-foot pass, Thorung La. Near Manang, vast pine forests cling to the north slopes of the Annapurna massif. These could supply a sustained yield for decades. But in this most remote corner of Nepal, the government is building an airstrip, so that tourists will be able to fly directly to Manang. What will happen to a culture bred by isolation is anybody's guess.

The Manangbhots have a wide and well-deserved reputation for being inhospitable, and their village has not a single hotel or teahouse. They have made no effort to share their culture with foreigners, as the Sherpas have done. Their Tibeto-Burman language is unwritten and almost unstudied. Even the name "Manang" is used inaccurately by other Nepalis. It correctly applies only to one village. Outsiders call the inhabitants of that village "Manangbhots," adding a suffix derived from "Bhotia"—a person of Tibetan ancestry. The people of Manang call themselves Nyeshang, and use the same name for their valley as well. To the rest of Nepal, however, Manang has become the name of the village, the valley, and a vast political district composed of several valleys.

A comparison of the Manangbhots and the Sherpas raises some intriguing questions. Both are lamaistic Buddhists of Tibetan ancestry who live at high altitude in the shadow of very high mountains. Both have lived partly from agriculture and partly from trade. Why, with such a common background, are they so different? Why are Manangbhots the most inhospitable and greedy of

mountain peoples, while the Sherpas are famous for generosity and selflessness?

The Manangbhots are proof that the Sherpas' unique qualities have not come from the simple sources romanticized in so many Himalayan writings. A Westerner who seeks to become like a Sherpa by thrusting himself into a nest of Buddhism in the high mountains could turn out more like a Manangbhot!

Both groups live in remote, inhospitable mountain environments that compel them to look beyond agriculture for a livelihood. The roots of their differences are in what they have done to fill that need.

For the Sherpas, local trade with Tibet involving travel no farther than Lhasa, Kathmandu, and Darjeeling was enough. When the trade ceased, tourism filled the gap. The Manangbhots are not as well situated for local trade, and they live in a colder, drier climate. Since their district has a shorter growing season and less rain than exists at similar elevations in the Khumbu, they never had the chance to strike the balance between home culture and trade that nurtured the selfless, yet strongly independent, ways of the Sherpas. The balance of their lives was tipped away from reliance on their home district and more toward distant trading. Although the local trade with Tibet through Central Nepal was enormous, it was controlled by the Thakalis who lived along the Kali Gandaki Gorge.

The Manang Valley—unlike the Khumbu—had access by broad trails suitable for men on horseback. Sherpas would have to walk great distances on foot to leave their homeland. Manangbhots could ride to the plains in four days. They became long-distance traders who took such things as musk, hides, silver, and turquoise to places as far away as Tibet, China, and Ceylon, where they swapped them for gems and silk. Their right to travel was formalized in 1789 when King Rana Bahadur Shah decreed them special privileges; today they have unrestricted visas and unusual export and import rights.

Centuries ago, the Manangbhots' contacts with the outside world led them to give up the prohibition on killing and hunting held by other Buddhist cultures. By the 1950s, the Manang Valley was in a state of anarchy because of feuds between Braga and Manang in which guns were used freely and many men were killed.

While it is clear that a human visitor feels more welcome in the Khumbu than in Manang, wildlife is a different story. One would think that wildlife would be safer among the Sherpas in a national park in the Khumbu than among the armed people of Manang, but such is not always the case. Although Sherpas are nonviolent and Manangbhots hunt and kill, the status of wildlife in the two areas is not very different.

Take the most hunted creature in the Himalaya, the musk deer. A Western trophy hunter would be embarrassed to bring one home, for it looks like a jackalope—a Rocky Mountain practical joke created by mounting antelope horns on a jackrabbit head. The musk deer stands two feet high at the shoulder, and weighs about 25 pounds. It has large hind legs, short forelegs, big ears, and it moves with a hopping gait. This most primitive of Asian deer has tusks instead of antlers. A gland on the underbelly of males contains about 1½ ounces of musk that is used in perfumes, oriental medicines, and aphrodisiacs; in 1977 one musk gland was worth four times its weight in gold, or enough to sustain a Nepali family for a year. Until the National Park and Wildlife Conservation Act of 1973 made it illegal to kill the deer, musk was Nepal's third largest

Upper left
Juniper patches at 14,000 feet, perhaps a thousand years old, burned by porters to keep warm.
Upper right
Hillside of burned juniper on Thorung La, caused by a porter fire getting out of control on a windy night.
Left
A yak caravan bearing firewood across the arid steppes north of Annapurna

export. Since then, the black market has raised the price and the trade is flourishing.

The deer live in forests at 7,000 to 14,000 feet. In winter and spring, when they descend to forage, they are most easily hunted. At that time, the men of Manang are away trading; they may deal in musk, but more often as middlemen than as harvesters. Few Sherpas poach directly, but they are not averse to receiving baksheesh from Tamangs and other Nepalis who do not share their Buddhist prohibition on the act of killing. Because of the renowned Sherpa tolerance of outsiders, bands of poachers find the Khumbu a far more attractive hunting ground than Manang, where they are not accepted and the musk habitat is not as concentrated.

Elsewhere in Nepal, the musk deer are caught by barricades of thorns several miles long. At strategic intervals, gates are booby-trapped with nooses; up to a thousand gates have been set in a single square mile of valley. On steeper hillsides the deer are hunted with dogs, bows, or guns. In western Nepal, one group of poachers placed poisoned spears on the ground and drove the musk deer toward them by setting fire to grassland and forest. In two months, they killed 105 deer and obtained 22 ounces of musk; all but one deer out of six were females or young that bore no musk. On the black market the musk was worth about 55,000 rupees, giving each of the men a lump sum equal to the yearly income of a porter who has been lucky enough to work 120 days for trekking groups.

There are no realistic solutions to the musk problem. Some experts advise a method of milking the musk that will not kill the animal. This would work if the musk trade was legal, but since live capture is far more difficult and attracts more attention, poachers will continue to kill. Other experts advise domestic musk deer farming, which the Chinese have already tried with some success. Many people fear that this will only sustain the trade in musk and create an ever-increasing market that will prove counterproductive to the survival of the wild species.

The solution most appealing to Western minds is to advocate the use of synthetic substitutes instead of musk in perfumes and medicines. Yet the application of science to musk and related substances may in the future create an even greater demand for the natural substance.

Strong ties between emotions, odors, and memory have been documented in many forms of life. Musk, like a mating lure to a moth or a scent on a hydrant to a dog, may trigger predictable reactions in humans. Controlled experiments have already shown that daily contact with musk shortens women's menstrual cycles. Further evidence that musk use is more than just Oriental hocuspocus will increase hunting pressure on an already-threatened species.

The first serious studies of wildlife in the Himalaya came 125 years after Hooker's observations. George Schaller, whose earlier studies of the gorilla, the African lion, and the Bengal tiger placed him at the apex of his field, concluded his three years of Himalayan field research with this observation:

"Man is modifying the world so fast and so drastically that most animals cannot adapt to the new conditions. In the Himalaya as elsewhere there is a great dying, one infinitely sadder than the Pleistocene extinctions, for man now has the knowledge and the need to save those remnants of his past."

Right
Aerial view of typical Nepali hill country
Far right
Another aerial including a Royal forest preserve, showing the enormous amount of cutting done by the native people

9 | On the Annapurna Trail

We walked through the dark stone alleys of Manang until a gate delivered us onto terraced fields at dawn. Horses grazed against a backdrop of ice, sky, and a green glacial lake. Stone fences that stretched across the fields seemed to mimic the moraines and fluted snow ridges of the Annapurna massif. Our footsteps led away from these spectacular heights into the Trans-Himalaya, a rounded and formidably barren world. By noon we had reached open highlands above all tree life except for junipers that clung crablike to the earth in low, tangled mats.

I became intrigued by the frequency of burned juniper patches. At least a third of the juniper patches we passed were totally blackened. Tsering, our sirdar, explained that native people crossed the pass between Manang and Muktinath in a single day; traveling with trekkers required an overnight stop. Porters hired for treks to Manang spent all but one night of the trip in comfortable places where low elevation or the nearness of a village precluded their need to bring heavy clothing and blankets. On the pass they simply huddled around a juniper patch and set it on fire, never considering that juniper near timberline can take more than a thousand years to regenerate.

As we crested a rise, we came face to face with an entire black hillside, embers smoldering. The mile-wide swath gradually narrowed until it stopped at trailside, where a juniper patch had been tindered on a windy night.

The silent stone village of Manang

Late in the afternoon, as Kim, Carl, and I walked the last steps into camp at 14,400 feet in a narrow canyon, we spotted a herd of wild sheep high above us. The porters and the rest of the group were still behind, and the creatures seemed unconcerned about our presence, especially since a nearly vertical wall of mud and rock separated their patch of meadow from the trail. With the wind direction and layout of the cliff perfect for a stalk, I was able to climb to the edge of the meadow without being seen. My pulse raced as I photographed them running across the skyline in evening light. Handholding a 400-mm lens, I concentrated on pushing the shutter button between heartbeats.

Black patches on the animals' forelegs and goatlike faces identified them as rare Tibetan blue sheep (*Pseudois nayaur*), also known as *bharal*. Blue sheep have become a scientific curiosity because they are a transitional species with characteristics of both goats and sheep. Their bodies, however, often make yet another species transition as they pass through yawning jaws to become part of the lithe form of a snow leopard. Blue sheep to leopards are like grains of rice to Nepali hill farmers: a chief food source, the object of a continual search that consumes most of life's energy and direction.

The next day's walking was by far the hardest of the trek. The trail wound relentlessly up to the 17,700-foot Thorung La. We found a sterility beyond any expectation. There were only piles of rock, devoid of life, as if the world's largest strip mine had just ceased operations. Higher, we entered the alpine zone where snowy peaks rose above the rocky matrix. South of the pass was 21,773-foot Thorungtse, draped with glacial ice. This was the peak that Kim, Vern, and I intended to climb.

Jo and I reached the pass, Thorung La, in four hours from 14,400 by walking at a slow, even pace. We had lunch with the group on the pass and then parted. Jo joined the group headed for Muktinath, and I stayed at the pass with the group that was going to climb Thorungtse.

There were six of us: Kim, Carl, Vern, me, a Sherpa (Ang Tende), and one Gurkha porter. Our goal was to climb the 21,000-foot north peak; the main summit was off limits. We planned to do the climb with day packs and catch up with the main group at Muktinath the same evening. We would start early the next morning. An oval lake on the pass gleamed with blue ice set off by white concentric rings, blending into the dark rock like a finely cut piece of turquoise. No winter snows had fallen yet, and we set up camp on the far shore.

The temperature dropped radically as soon as the sun went behind Thorungtse. We switched from shirtsleeves to down jackets and gloves. When the ill-dressed Gurkha porter began shivering, Carl gave him his own down jacket to use for the night and then took off to catch the group at Muktinath. With Carl gone, there were five of us. We went to bed and slept fitfully, unused to the sudden altitude change and wondering how it would be to climb far higher the next day. Vern awoke with enough of a headache that he decided not to join us. Also, his single boots seemed inadequate for the cold and snow. By six in the morning Kim and I were off, staggering through knee-deep snow, unsure whether we had the energy to climb high in such conditions.

After a few hundred feet the snow changed to hard windslab. We put on our crampons and began to move at great speed. Each easy kick sunk our front points firmly to the hilt. We felt no need for the rope, because of our confidence in ourselves and each other. The two of us moved at the same rate, feeling the same needs. There was no discussion when we finally came to a place where we roped for an icy traverse across a fifty-five-degree bulge. It was as if one mind and one body were climbing in two places at once, connected by an invisible thread. This joy of moving together as one was central to our deepest mountain experience. We experienced intuitive sharing, intuitive support, and outward individuality—a perfect society.

We were surprised when the angle of the slope eased and we crested the summit ridge. At 10:30 A.M. we stood on a plateau the size of a city block, higher than any point around us except the south summit, to which we were connected by a corniced ridge that dropped out of sight into the gap. The great peak of Annapurna came into view for the first time from a rarely seen angle. Its sloping north wall appeared vertical. Winds in excess of 100 mph were ripping snow from its ridges and blowing plumes hundreds of feet into the air, an indication that the seasonal lowering of the jet stream had already occurred.

On Thorungtse the air was perfectly still. The Great Barrier, which prevented access to Annapurna from the east or north, was in full view—an unbroken fifteen-mile wall over 20,000 feet high. And in the opposite direction, the north, was Mustang, a barren valley of reddish-brown earth set between rows of white peaks. Somewhere out there was Lo Mantang, the walled capital city of Mustang, visited by fewer than a dozen Westerners in history. We felt a sense of mystery far deeper than if we had been looking at Lhasa, for Mustang has never been open to foreigners. While travel to Tibet was allowed in prewar days, Mustang remained a separate kingdom, ruled by a rajah. Since 1951 Mustang has been included within Nepal's boundary, but it has maintained its autonomy in a feudatory relationship with the King of Nepal. Every year trekking companies advertise the first walks into Mustang, and every year the trips are cancelled because the rumored opening does not happen.

After twenty minutes on top we started down, practically running in our crampons. Shortly after noon we arrived at the pass, where Ang Tende served us a hot lunch. Vern had just returned from exploring the rocky slopes of neighboring Yakhawa up to 20,000 feet. The three of us switched to running shoes, broke camp, and skipped down the trail to Muktinath. To have been at 21,000 feet in the late morning and to be at 12,000 feet in a warm village by two in the afternoon was an amazingly broad experience for a single day on foot. We burst with joy and good feelings until we reached the outskirts of the village.

A European couple, nattily dressed in wool knickers and embroidered knee socks, sauntered down the path in front of us. As we caught up, I said "Hello!" in a cheerful voice. The woman turned, looked through us as if we weren't there, and kept walking without a word. I assumed she spoke no English.

When we reached a Hindu pagoda in the grove of cottonwoods, Jo ran to greet me with a hug and kiss. I was covered with dust from running on the trail, and she decided that I should have a bath. With hot water from the camp and cold water from the stream, I emerged clean, refreshed, and ready for a visit to the holy shrines.

Ang Tsering led us into the Buddhist gompa, where we peered through a tattered curtain at flames burning on water. For Buddhists, this was the most holy place in Nepal outside the Kathmandu Valley. Jo and I went on alone to the Hindu shrine, where 108 fountains poured forth holy waters. Following the custom of the pilgrims, I began to anoint myself with water from each spout. A voice called out in perfect English, "Move to the right. I want to take a picture!"

*Porters below
Annapurna South
on the lush
southern side
of the range.*

The European lady I had met on the path appeared with a battery of Japanese optics. I retreated silently with gritted teeth.

Gerry had a similar experience. While he quietly watched a Buddhist service in the gompa, a group of Europeans tromped in and loudly discussed what they saw, treating the living pilgrims as if they were objects in a museum. They were part of a trekking group camped only a hundred yards from us. After the two incidents, we avoided contact with them.

When dinner was served in our large kitchen tent, Kim and Carl arrived thoroughly soused after several rounds of rakshi at a nearby teahouse. After dinner they bought another round and returned to the tent, where they laughed and joked into the night. Carl made a foray for more rakshi and found the teahouse closed. He asked Tsering to find him more rakshi, and Tsering gently urged him to go to bed. Instead, Carl returned to the tent. Minutes later we heard a tremendous metallic noise. The entire portable table for nine—complete with pots, pans, dishes, and silver—had gone into the air. Tsering asked for my help when Carl came out demanding rakshi yet again. When I went to talk to Carl, he put his arm around me like a big, friendly bear, pulled out a wad of bills, and tried to enlist me into his pursuit of booze. It took all the self-control I could muster not to point at the lantern glowing in the next camp and say, "Carl, I'm sure they have some rakshi!"

Carl went to sleep without additional rakshi. The incident had been contained only because Muktinath had limited liquor supplies, and was not yet geared to the tourist trade.

We arose to see the blue-white bulk of Dhaulagiri profiled against the glow of the rising sun. Twelve easy miles of downhill walking brought us to the big village of Jomosom on the floor of the Kali Gandaki gorge. Culture shock was instantaneous. Children asked for chocolate. Adults held out their palms for rupees or cigarettes. Carl stopped for refueling at a hotel that sold bottled liquor.

Jomosom is sixty-five miles from the nearest road, but it has had strong Western influence for decades. In 1977, 5,119 trekkers were given permits to visit Jomosom and hundreds of airborne visitors arrived by scheduled flights in Twin Otter airplanes. I was glad that we were not spending the night in Jomosom, but continuing the three miles to Marpha.

Walking the Kali Gandaki can be one of the world's most miserable hiking experiences. The lowest passage through the Himalayan crest for hundreds of miles, it serves as a pressure equalizer between the Indian subcontinent and Eurasia. Typically, fierce gusts of wind begin at ten in the morning and scour the canyon floor for the remainder of the day. We walked straight into a ground blizzard of dirt, sand, and yak dung. I found it hard to believe that just the day before I had been standing on pure snow in still air at 21,000 feet.

Marpha's walls and narrow alleys offered respite from the wind and the people of the town seemed far less jaded by tourism than their neighbors at Jomosom. From our Sherpas, however, we learned a disturbing story. Just a few months earlier, a European trekking group had passed through on a similar trek around Annapurna, when a drunken Khamba came near their camp. The Sherpas tried to keep him away. One Sherpa was stabbed to death near a great white rock by the river. The morning after the incident, the Khamba was discovered broken and lifeless on the trail. Sherpas may advocate nonviolence, but loyalty to each other takes precedence.

Kim and Carl planned to split from the group the next morning and make a side trip to the Annapurna Sanctuary. They set off early, and we sauntered through the heart of Kali Gandaki behind them, passing between Annapurna and Dhaulagiri at an elevation of only 7,500 feet. That night we camped in a pine forest near Lete in sight of Annapurna. We had an especially fine dinner of fried fish, potatoes, cauliflower fried in butter, pumpkin sauce, soup, and tea. Most of the items had been purchased locally. The Sherpas sang and danced for us, and we sang them American songs. We had not had such an evening before because of the lack of firewood and the Sherpas' fear that festivities with Carl might get out of hand.

Jo asked Tsering how the stress of modern life had affected the Sherpas. He replied that there were no words for stress or depression in their language. They believed that, when necessary, god would intervene on their behalf. Even educated Sherpas retained a strong vestige of this belief, making it come true for others by their own generosity. Not knowing the pitfalls of progress, they were ready to welcome technology with open arms. Only geographical isolation had so far kept electricity, roads, and motors out of their homeland.

The following day we paralleled the Kali Gandaki River's descent next to tremendous cataracts and waterfalls. We suddenly emerged from alpine into tropical vegetation. Our itinerary said, "We'll camp at the village of Tatopani, famous for its mineral springs (just right for a soothing hot bath)."

Entering the village, Jo and I passed open shops stocked with everything from tennis shoes to beer, but the place seemed like a ghost town. Then we heard loud noises coming from a distant building and saw a large crowd gathered. Long before we reached the scene, we knew the source of the noise. We were hearing the same frenzied howl that had pierced the air just before the camp table was upended in Muktinath.

Inside a thatched-roof teahouse, Carl and Kim were reeling around with open bottles of Khukri rum. At the table was the mayor of the village, head nestled in empty bottles. The Nepalese Army was in Tatopani on a recruiting mission but the ranking officer was barely ambulatory, and his second in command lay motionless in the gutter with one arm pointed skyward like the rigid limb of a road-killed rabbit. The army doctor, a more conservative drinker, had stopped after the first half-dozen rounds and returned to examining inductees, mustering everyone from old men to hacking tubercular bone-racks.

Kim explained how the fear-and-loathing scene had come about. Carl's feet had begun to blister badly at the fast pace, so they stopped to wait for us rather than go on to the Sanctuary. Carl quickly befriended the town's authority figures and bought them endless rounds of drinks. Within hours, Tatopani was in chaos. Commerce could not have been stopped more surely had an earthquake occurred.

When we gathered in a courtyard for the night, our normally boisterous Gurkha porters sat strangely still with faraway looks in their eyes. They, too, were victims of Carl's generosity. A bottle of Khukri rum secretly laced with hash oil had turned them into zombies. We coaxed Carl into a hotel after paying the owner a large bribe and promising him that Sherpas would guard the door.

Our group was deeply embarrassed, and some of us reflected on the ugly and unwanted effects of mountain tourism. The undeveloped villages, such as Manang, are nearly immune to such problems as Yankee tourists tearing up their teahouses. They don't like tourists and so they don't have any teahouses for them. Tatopani, on the other hand, is a tourists' town, and it caters to their love of alcohol.

As in any other part of the world, easy availability of alcohol gives it a high degree of social acceptance. At Yosemite and Yellowstone parks in the United States, for example, it is not considered improper to have a few too many drinks at one of the bars. But drunks are far less common or tolerated in the back country. Even so, it is hardly a coincidence that Yosemite, with its easy availability of booze, has the highest crime rate and the most serious social problems of any park in the American System. In Nepal, Tatopani has developed similar attractions for the wild lushes from the West.

Tatopani means "hot springs." Before trekkers began to come, hot, clear water bubbled forth between boulders next to the river. Then the hot water was channeled into a large pool confined by four walls of concrete.

As Jo and I walked toward the promised waters, an English girl asked us the way, saying, "I've heard it's *the* place to wash your hair." We arrived to find a Frenchman washing his underwear with bar soap in a pool that now looked as if it were filled with curdled milk. We continued walking until we found a place where a shallow trickle of clear hot water joined the river. We soaked in splendor in a wild setting—not as good as the original Tatopani, but still a joy after days on the trail.

As we left Tatopani the next morning, I thought about all the little incidents concerning trekkers of other nationalities that I had recorded in my diary, and I wondered what tales they would bring home about the wild Americans who hooted and hollered at sacred Muktinath and turned peaceful Tatopani into an alcoholic side show. I also worried about the effects we had on the villagers. The Thakali people of the Kali Gandaki are far more likely to be changed by Westerners than other Nepali hill dwellers such as the Sherpas or Manangbhots. Their history is one of cultural and religious flexibility in order to reach economic goals. Long ago, they had compromised their Buddhist beliefs with a heavy mixture of Hinduism for the sake of trade with the orthodox Hindus of Kathmandu and India.

As we climbed out of the depths of the Kali Gandaki toward Ghorapani, the classic vision of Nepal returned. Great foothills, green as the California coast in spring, rolled toward white apparitions floating in the sky—the peaks of the Dhaulagiri Himal. Villages appeared at natural breaks in the landscape, populated by people who cared enough to grow marigolds, hang them from fences or bridges, and pass them to trekkers with no expectations of something in return. Dirt floors were cleanly swept, firewood neatly stacked. Life was complete without television, the pocket computer, or even the wheel.

After a long day's climb out of Tatopani, we camped a stone's throw from the center of Ghorapani in a clearing. Twisted rhododendron branches hid the mile drop into the Kali Gandaki and framed a perfect picture of the Annapurna Himal. At five in the morning, several of us hiked to the top of Poon Hill to witness the fabled 360-degree sunrise. Colors changed in every quadrant of the sky during the magic hour before golden shafts of light finally poked through a snowy gap and illuminated the south face of Dhaulagiri, a curtain of ice and rock the height of three Eigerwands. For the remainder of the morning we walked open fields along a ridge toward Deorali Pass, following a route to Pokhara that had little tourist impact.

Two days later we set foot in Pokhara, a place that confirmed Pogo's

Frozen lake
and the north peak
of Thorungtse

aphorism, "We have met the enemy and he is us!" Pokhara had been a quiet, unspoiled Nepali town until 1961, when it began to receive the blessings of mechanization. In reverse order from the rest of the world, its first motor vehicle was an airplane, and out of its fuselage came the second: a steamroller to ensure a smooth landing for Queen Elizabeth's impending visit. For a dozen more years, no road connected Pokhara to Kathmandu, eighty air miles away. Even so, jeeps and cars gradually proliferated. One of the last vehicles on the scene was the bicycle, followed soon after by Russian taxicabs and air-conditioned Mercedes buses that encapsulated European tourists on packaged tours.

Pokhara in the afternoon was an oppressively hot Asian city, teeming with people and odors. At dawn it was an entirely different place, a dark theater dominated by sunrise on the great peaks. Nowhere else in the Himalaya had we seen such vivid colors. Light rays which had passed near the earth over the Gangetic Plain with just a touch of gold had been filtered by miles of dusty air until only the purest shafts of red were left to strike the snows of Machha-puchhare and the Annapurna massif. Here was the eternal contrast of the Himalaya, the changeable and the unchangeable side by side, mountain and city, snow and sunlight, seen by trekkers who paid to walk in primitive style, then elbowed each other for seats on the airplane to Kathmandu. We took the same flight to Kathmandu, and then went our separate ways in twos and threes. Gerry, Jo, and I headed home.

The mixture of ancient ways and technology that we had witnessed in Pokhara were carried to an extreme in the Delhi airport. Air India had a fleet of new 747s, yet reservations were still scribbled on slips of paper and stuffed into compartments in a king-sized Lazy Susan that sat directly under a propeller-sized fan. It was little wonder that there were always more bookings than seats. Our flight had been confirmed in Kathmandu, yet our names were not on the passenger list. Along with forty-five other passengers, we were refused boarding on the overbooked flight.

To make matters worse, Indian immigration officials refused me a normal visa because of the technicality that I had visited the country in the last six months. I would have to leave the country within twenty-four hours, but the next flight—already full—was not in the next twenty-four hours. I could appeal the decision at the head office in town, but the office was closed on Sunday, and it was now Saturday night. I decided to take the twenty-four-hour visa and hope for the best.

Nearly a hundred passengers were overbooked for the next 747. The poor Air India manager was besieged by a ticket-waving jackal pack which howled threats as it followed him from office to office—even into the men's room. With nearly five hundred people waiting for one airplane in close quarters, the temperature and humidity were soon unbearable. In line in front of us a well-dressed couple from Los Angeles held first-class tickets. He was a musician. At first they chatted idly about classical music, but as the hours passed they became sullen and withdrawn. Their names were not on the passenger list, and the thought of going through the same scene yet again must have weighed heavily on their souls. The husband sat on his expensive luggage as if in a catatonic trance, ignoring beggars asking for alms and other passengers with questions.

A woman in a golden sari came wailing into the room. She knelt in front of

an Indian national who was holding a boarding pass, and began an amazing variety of anguished sobs, tears, and gestures accompanied by a repetitive, plaintive wail. She was pleading with her loved one not to leave the country.

The man in front of us suddenly came to life and turned to say something to his wife. I thought, of course, that he had been deeply moved by the emotional display. At first I didn't understand when I overheard him say, "G-F." His wife looked at him strangely and he repeated it again: "G-F. Just like in *Luccia*!" He was going through an experience that had taken away his ability for human compassion. A musician with perfect pitch, he had identified the tones in the woman's wail.

The positive side of the Delhi experience is that it keeps out casual visitors. Much of the charm and near-pristine condition of Nepal's mountains is due to the fact that dependable air service like that found in Europe and America does not exist. Only committed travelers seek out Nepal, a fact confirmed by the unusually long length of stay of the average tourist: 11.6 days in 1977. The eventual coming of reliable air service to Nepal will be as mixed a blessing as the building of a freeway into a national park.

Sunrise on Machapuchare from Pokhara

The Himalaya seen through the Sal forest of Royal Chitwan National Park from 125 miles away

For all its mystery, the Himalaya has no hidden pockets of wholly unique creatures. The isolation that greets human eyes today is too geologically recent to have permitted an alpine Galapagos to evolve. Quite the opposite occurred. The rise of the Himalaya, instead of separating regions, joined two great realms of the animal world for the first time.

The world's youngest major mountain range rose out of the collision of India and Eurasia after the Age of Mammals was well under way. Elsewhere on earth, mammals had expanded their ranges or evolved to populate existing mountains. The crest of the Himalaya, however, created a sharp boundary between the venerable Oriental and Palearctic realms. The ancestors of modern jungle animals came from ancient India and as migrants from Africa, while the forebears of present high-altitude residents came from the colder northern latitudes.

This overview is, of course, oversimplified. Some species are unique to the Himalaya, while others, like the tiger, have crossed the mountain barrier to foresake the Asian steppes of their evolution for the humid jungles. The northerly Palearctic region is circumpolar in extent, due to the ice ages. This accounts for the presence of such creatures as the brown bear, a member of the same species (*Ursus arctos*) as the North American grizzly. The wild sheep of the high mountains are relatives of the American bighorn, while the horned animals of the range's southern flanks are most commonly related to antelope or cattle.

Only two centuries ago, the Indian subcontinent surpassed Africa in the diversity of its large wildlife. Herds of ten thousand black buck swept over plains that are now flooded with people. Wildlife photography of existing creatures shows only a minor part of this heritage, that which has survived. Only a few small remnants remain of the vast Terai jungle that covered much of the Indo-Gangetic plain as recently as thirty years ago. The opening photos of this essay are from Royal Chitwan National Park in Nepal where a few tigers, Indian rhinos, and crocodiles survive within sight of the great peaks of the Annapurna Range. To put them into perspective, we must consider the habitat they have lost, and imagine in human terms a planet Earth reduced to one small habitable nation. The future for many Himalayan animals is desperately bleak. No one has described the final stage better than zoologist George Schaller, who wrote the following description of barren foothills in Pakistan at the end of five years of surveying Himalayan wildlife:*

The place has a derelict look, burned into submission by the sun. Forlorn camels drift down sandy streets between mud-walled homes, and the inhabitants scuttle like desert rodents across alleys from one burrow to the next . . . . One tends to accept the desolate scene as inevitable, the product of a desperate aridity, for the rainfall is only seven inches a year. But then one begins to better understand the landscape. Here and there stunted acacias have been cut and left to dry, to be picked up later and sold for firewood . . . . Herds of black-haired goats, thin bony creatures, scour the terrain, leaving only thorny and ill-tasting plants in their wake. Had man not misused this land for thousands of years, I would be driving through woodland, with wild asses standing in the broad-crowned shade of acacias and cheetah stalking unsuspecting Indian gazelle through swards of golden grass. Perhaps down by the river a pride of lions would be resting after the night's hunt. The forests are gone now, the rivers dry except after a downpour, and the lion, cheetah, and asses are dead. Only a few gazelle remain. No wonder the land seems lonely as one drives toward the distant hills, trailing a funnel of red dust made incandescent by the sun.

Right
*Bengal tiger eating a buffalo
calf. Photographed by
spotlight at night.
(All photos these two pages
taken in Royal Chitwan
National Park, Nepal.)*

Above
Himalayan fishing eagle
Right
One-horned Asian rhinoceros

Left
Marsh crocodile
Below
Chital or axis Deer

Manaslu from fir forest
in the Marsyandi
Valley,
Nepal

Upper left
The Himalayan griffon,
Nepal's largest
bird, has been
described as
"a starving bundle
of feathers
and nerves
looking for
something dead."
Upper right
Barn owl, Kathmandu

Center
Sunrise from
Poon Hill
over the
Kali Gandaki gorge.
Bottom
Kestrel falcon,
Khumbu region,
Nepal

10 | From the Alps to the Karakoram

The old adage that history repeats itself seems especially true in the mountains of the world. Mountaineers are travelers, and it is hardly surprising that we find the same names and similar deeds in the Alps, the Andes, and the Himalaya. There is a marked similarity between events in the Himalaya since World War II and in the European Alps roughly a century before.

The major mountains of both the Alps and the Himalaya remained unclimbed until "alpinists" arrived from afar and hired as porters or guides the people who lived within sight of the peaks. These native people were farmers and herdsmen who quickly discovered that mountain tourism offered an escape from the rigid social and economic hierarchies of their cultures. Peasants became Swiss guides; hill farmers turned into Sherpa sirdars. With their assistance, "impossible" summits were reached. Both areas had "golden ages" of roughly a decade during which the most important summits were ascended for the first time. In the Alps this period lasted from the 1854 ascent of the Wetterhorn to the 1865 ascent of the Matterhorn. During the corresponding Himalayan period, 1950 to 1960, all fourteen 8,000-meter (26,262-foot) summits were climbed for the first time. The highest peaks fell like dominoes: Mount Everest in 1953, K2 in 1954, Kanchenjunga in 1955, Lhotse in 1956.

In both the Alpine and Himalayan periods, returning adventurers wrote books, gave lectures, and were interviewed for magazines and newspapers. Predictably, the public became interested in experiencing the wonder and

Primroses at 17,000 feet in the Karakoram Himalaya, Pakistan

mystery of the mountains for itself. By 1870, many villagers in the Alps had begun to orient their lives around mountain tourism. Huts were built within a day's walk of every major Alpine summit. A tourist could walk between huts while climbers used them as bases for mountain ascents. Local people worked as guides, porters, and hutkeepers in the mountains; others served the tourists in hotels and restaurants in the valleys.

Nepal is headed in the direction of the Alps. New hotels and teahouses are proliferating in the high valleys. Native people are gearing up for tourism. Lodges a day's walk apart may become the way of the future, enabling city people from all over the world to view Mount Everest from 18,000 feet, so long as they are physically fit enough to move along a well-signed trail for a few hours each day. The result of such a trend will not necessarily be a Disneyland of the mountains; it is more likely to resemble Switzerland: beautiful, symmetrical, formal, and predictable. Visitors will move on foot through manicured, semiwild terrain rather than by vehicle in the motorized malignancy so characteristic of American parks. Such a repetition of what happened in the Alps a century ago is only made possible by Nepal's lack of roads and modern communications, which very much resemble the situation in Europe in the nineteenth century.

The remarkable similarities between Nepal and the Alps are much more than a cross-pollination of mountain cultures. Current interest in trekking and climbing in Nepal has been spread almost entirely by the written word, and those words have been turned into a self-fulfilling prophecy by constant repetition of the erroneous belief that climbing mountains began in Europe and spread to the rest of the world. Techniques of roped climbing did indeed spread around the world from the Alps. However, this in no way means that mountain climbing or mountain walking have their roots in Europe.

This view simply ignores the actions of native people in their home mountains and places undue emphasis on European achievement and the Alpine example. For example, Eric Newby in his 1977 book, *Great Ascents*, describes Younghusband's 1887 crossing of Mustagh Pass as "one of the great and courageous exploits of these early days." Omitted are the more commonplace acts of the native people who lived on both sides of this 18,000-foot pass. They used it for centuries, brought horses and yaks across it, fought wars over it, and even set up an 800-foot-long polo field high on the south side to have intermountain competitions.

Farther afield, the Atacama Indians reached a 22,000-foot summit in the Andes before 1550 A.D., higher than Lord Conway's claimed world altitude recorded in 1892. And obsidian flakes found on the summit plateau of Mount Whitney, the highest point in the contiguous United States, indicate that Indians climbed the peak long ago.

Some historians try to hold onto the Alps as the source of "mountain sport" by claiming that earlier ascents of mountains in other areas had a purpose, whereas the birth of climbing for its own sake—sport—was in the Alps. But it is far easier to impute a purpose to the first ascent of the Matterhorn (fame) than to the ascent of 19,000-foot Kilimanjaro by a solitary leopard, high above its element, or to the ascent of glacier-draped Mount Rainier by a black bear. The pursuit of places higher than one's normal realm may be almost universal among intelligent creatures. Is there a purpose to an eagle's flight so far above the earth that he can no longer spot prey?

In America, neither mountaineering nor mountain recreation have closely followed the example of the Alps. We are removing from our national parks the same sorts of structures that are being built in Nepal. Our high mountains are surrounded by wilderness, not by hut systems, cable cars, and hotels. The Alpine example didn't fit in America because we lacked a preexisting culture of mountain people who were willing to reorient their lives around the deeds of newcomers on their local summits.

With this background of how the Alpine example has affected other regions, we are ready to move our focus to Pakistan and the Karakoram Himalaya. Here is a land very different from Nepal. It is significantly farther north, and much of its area is above 10,000 feet, where agriculture is not feasible. Mount Everest rises directly out of the fields of the Khumbu, but K2 in the Karakoram is a seventy-mile trek from the nearest habitation. The scenic grandeur of the uninhabited Karakoram valleys is at least equal to that of Nepal, but there is not a single hut, hotel, or teahouse. Trekking with native porters is far more expensive than in Nepal, both because the wages are four times as high and because many more men must be hired to carry food for both trekkers and porters through the uninhabited regions. For instance, on a twenty-day excursion a porter would need to carry two pounds of food per day for his own needs. Working within the government-set load limit of fifty-five pounds, and considering that five of those are used up in sacks or containers, he is only able to carry ten pounds of payload.

In most other parts of the Himalaya, trekking is more a cultural than a wilderness experience. The trails are ancient and well traveled, and they connect villages that are often within sight of one another. The mountains are high islands of wildness rising out of populated and cultivated valleys. People who have spent time in true wilderness mountains, such as the Alaska Range or the North Cascades, are often disappointed that their "dream trip" through the earth's ultimate mountain range parallels human settlements and effects upon the land.

Trekking has yet to become popular in the Karakoram, and it is highly unlikely that it will ever follow the example of either Nepal or Switzerland. Although a subrange of the Himalaya, the Karakoram is nearly a thousand miles northwest of Everest, a distance equal to that from the Grand Canyon to Vancouver, British Columbia. In this case, however, it is the more northerly area that is arid. The crest of the Himalaya forms a climatic wall that effectively makes the Karakoram a convoluted Sahara. Its valleys are dusty and for the most part treeless. Unlike monsoon-drenched Nepal, the Karakoram has no surplus of food in the high valleys to feed a large influx of tourists, and there is no way to bring food from outside except on the backs of men.

Indo-Pakistani border conflicts in Kashmir kept the Karakoram closed to outsiders from 1960 to 1974. Since 1975, it has been the most active Himalayan region in terms of mountaineering, but the quietest in terms of trekking. Statistics for 1977 showed that Nepal had twenty-eight expeditions to major peaks and 17,000 trekkers while the Karakoram had forty expeditions but only sixty trekkers in the uninhabited mountains above the highest villages.

The decade and a half of the Karakoram closure saw a greater increase in world mountaineering activity and accomplishment than in all previous history. A new generation of climbers was waiting to pounce on the unclimbed challenges of the range. The region surrounding K2 has both more high peaks

Above
*Aerial view of
Paiyu-Trango area:
Nanga Parbat
on skyline.*
Left
*Gasherbrum IV,
the most symmetrical
of the world's
26,000-foot mountains.
Gasherbrum II is on
the right skyline
in this telephoto
from the
Baltoro Glacier.*
Right
*Gasherbrum IV,
Hidden Peak and the
Baltoro Glacier from
the summit of
Great Trango Tower*

in a concentrated area and a higher mean elevation than any place on earth. Nineteen expeditions from Austria, Poland, America, France, Italy, England, Switzerland, and Japan converged on the same approach to the mountains between May and July of 1975. The coveted peaks were those above the Baltoro and the Biafo glaciers, which drained into the Braldu River. In the river canyon reposed a handful of very primitive villages populated by Muslim Baltis. Their strong backs were the key to the passage of every expedition, since the use of private aircraft was forbidden by the government, and pack animals could not be used to traverse trailless canyon walls or cross great torrents spanned by bridges woven from willow twigs. Every one of these modern expeditions had to run its efficient machine through the ancient, handmade gears of the Balti culture. The result was chaos.

The Balti people appeared to be simple folk locked somewhere between the Stone Age and medieval times. They had managed to survive under the rule of one conqueror or another for more than a thousand years, always far enough from the sources of power that direct pressures on their lives were sporadic. They had a deep fear of authority, but also an irresistible urge to outwit it. To them, an expedition was another form of officialdom.

With careful organization, the Baltis could have supplied the manpower to move all the 1975 expeditions to their base camps. Instead, they chose their own brand of collective bargaining. The government had set a single wage to be paid each porter for each day's work from the 8,000-foot valleys to the 17,000-foot base camps. As soon as they left the warm valleys and began to walk over ice, they simply sat down on the job, knowing that they held all the cards. The expedition couldn't hire other porters in the wilderness above the highest village. Neither could it transport its own gear. Unless unusually high wages were paid, along with gifts of equipment, the Baltis would quit one expedition in midstream and walk back to carry for another for the same wage at lower altitudes. Several expeditions gave up before reaching their base camps. Others went on to their mountain after long delays and with limited supplies. Still others paid the demands, caused local inflation, and returned home tens of thousands of dollars in debt.

In fairness to the Baltis, their situation was quite different from that of other Himalayan peoples. Expeditions to the Karakoram were generally larger than those to other parts of the Himalaya because of the vast uninhabited distances to be covered and the great height of the peaks. Charles Bruce, a member of the first mountaineering expedition to the Karakoram in 1892 and leader of two later expeditions to Everest, summed up the Baltis' plight: "What would have happened a hundred years ago in Switzerland if a whole village had been ordered to send every available man with some unknown Englishman and to stay with him for a fortnight above the snow-line?"

Before World War II, Karakoram expeditions traditionally used hundreds of local Baltis as porters, but they imported Sherpas from Nepal to work above base camp on the mountain itself. Sherpas who lived in Darjeeling were free to commute while the Karakoram was part of India. The division of the subcontinent and subsequent splitting of Kashmir put the Karakoram under Pakistani control; Sherpas were not allowed into Pakistan.

Post-war expeditions were faced with two alternatives: employ high porters from Baltistan and Hunza who lacked the Sherpas' mountain skills, or try to climb entirely without their aid. The first two expeditions to visit the heart of the Karakoram after the war both attempted K2, but the difference in their styles was revealing. Charles Houston's 1953 American expedition went without oxygen and used no porters above 20,500 feet; they hired 125 Baltis to transport food and gear to base camp. In contrast, Ardito Desio's 1954 effort brought oxygen and used ten Hunza high porters and 700 regular porters. Houston's light expedition failed; Desio's expedition made the first ascent of K2. Coming only a year after the success of an equally ponderous expedition on Everest, Desio's triumph tended to reinforce the belief that big expeditions were necessary to climb big mountains.

A closer look at the two expeditions shows little difference in the solidity of their positions high on the mountain. All eight members of Houston's team reached a camp at 25,000 feet with a ten-day supply of food. They failed because of a series of unusual events. One climber—Art Gilkey—became critically ill with thrombophlebitis just as the greatest summer storm in years hit K2. His companions tried to help him, but on the way down he was swept away in an avalanche and the climb was abandoned. Desio's huge effort placed the same number of men at a similar elevation, eight at 25,400 feet, but without as much food and fuel. Their success came from a last-ditch effort that cost a Hunza high porter the front halves of both feet. With good health and weather, Houston's team would have had an equal chance to make the first ascent of K2 without oxygen. If it had happened that way, and if climbers had accepted the conclusion to be drawn from it—that high summits could be reached by light parties without oxygen—the next quarter-century of high-altitude mountaineering might have had an entirely different thrust. The great expeditions, with their locustlike effects upon the land, might not have dominated high-altitude endeavors.

The American K2 climbers of 1953 were strong men with outstanding backgrounds on snow and ice. Rock climbing, however, was still in an embryonic state in America. The faces of Half Dome and El Capitan in Yosemite were completely unclimbed, as were most of the steep walls in the Cascades, the Sierra, and the Rocky Mountains. When these men saw the granite peaks of the lower Baltoro Glacier, they were awestruck. To climb such precipices, even at moderate altitudes, was beyond their wildest dreams. Bob Craig looked at the Trango Towers and wrote, "These are hardly mountains; they are fantasies of the imagination . . . blocks of rock, often capped with ice, rise vertically for 8,000 feet, for all the world like mammoth skyscrapers."

British climbers returning from a successful climb of 23,860-foot Mustagh Tower in 1956 had a different feeling about the towers. One of them, Joe Brown, was not only the top rock climber in Britain and perhaps all of Europe, but also a veteran of high-altitude climbing who had made the first ascent of Kanchenjunga, the world's third highest peak, just the previous summer. He realized that these granite towers offered him a unique chance to combine his talents, and he vowed to come back.

In 1957 a tiny Austrian expedition came to the Karakoram to try an 8,000-meter peak without oxygen or high-altitude porters. Hermann Buhl, Fritz Wintersteller, Markus Schmuck, and Kurt Diemberger made the first ascent of 26,400-foot Broad Peak entirely under their own power, spending nearly a month ferrying their supplies up the mountain until they were within striking distance of the summit. The climb caused a sensation in the mountaineering world, but it had surprisingly little effect on the constant parade of big expeditions bound for the Himalaya. Buhl, who had a reputation as a superman, died on Chogolisa immediately after the Broad Peak climb. What he did on Broad Peak was considered more a godlike feat than an example to be followed by mortals.

In 1958, a medium-sized American expedition climbed Hidden Peak. The 26,470-foot mountain became the only one of the world's fourteen 8,000-meter peaks first ascended by Americans. The leader, Nick Clinch, became captivated by the sight of Paiyu Peak, a spectacular tiered pyramid of red granite and ice that flanked the Baltoro Glacier near the Trango Towers. His dream of climbing it was cut short by the region's closure.

When the Karakoram closed in 1960, almost no multiday technical climbs had been made in any of the world's remote mountain areas. The big walls of Alaska, Baffin Island, and Patagonia were virtually untouched. By the time the Karakoram reopened in 1974 the emphasis in mountaineering had shifted away from the mere gaining of summits or absolute altitudes toward style. Throughout the world, new ways were being sought up old climbs, and routes previously classed as impossible were becoming standard fare. Many climbers, however, believed that the new techniques would not be useful at extreme altitudes.

In 1975, Hidden Peak had a second ascent that combined all the modern trends of style into a single effort. Two climbers from Tyrol (an area politically part of Italy but culturally more Austrian) attempted a new route on this 8,000-meter peak with no high-altitude porters, no fixed ropes, no fixed camps, and no oxygen. The climbing team, Reinhold Messner and Peter Habeler, used only twelve porters to transport their food and equipment up the Baltoro Glacier; then they acclimatized for two weeks before giving the mountain everything they had. Beginning from a 19,356-foot col, they climbed an ice face with light packs and bivouacked at 23,300; they reached the 26,470-foot summit shortly after noon on the second day.

Before the war, their route had been dismissed by Himalayan experts as too difficult. A giant French expedition in 1936 had floundered on an easier-appearing ridge after months of effort; their equipment was brought in by 850 porters.

Messner and Habeler's climb, instead of reaching near the limits of the possible (as some conservative mountaineers suggested), opened new horizons for technically skilled climbers, who were a hundred-fold more numerous than a decade earlier. It put a final stamp of authenticity on what had once been a remote vision: that difficult terrain at Himalayan altitudes could be climbed without an umbilical cord connected to a mass of people and equipment. And it hinted that the cord was less of a guarantee of safety than a ball and chain holding free men prisoners at the bases of walls they were fully capable of scaling.

With the sudden reopening of the Karakoram in 1974 came the first expeditions to the "low-altitude" granite peaks next to the Baltoro Glacier—Paiyu Peak, Uli Biaho Tower, the Grand Cathedral, and the Trango Towers—all between 19,000 and 22,000 feet. Conventional expeditions to the big peaks usually took a year or two to organize, fund, mobilize, and staff. Alpine-style efforts to these lower peaks could be mobilized with not much more than the gear in a climber's basement, a day's planning, and a good portion of his life's savings. Thus, the summer of 1974 brought attempts on Paiyu Peak and Uli

Biaho Tower, but no attempts on the region's former attractions: the six peaks over 26,000 feet.

The prize of the Trangos was a symmetrical shaft known as Nameless Tower. It rose vertically on all sides for at least 2,500 feet above a base that was already 5,000 feet above the Baltoro Glacier. Over the years, passing mountaineers had labeled it "impossible," "inaccessible," and "the ultimate rock climb."

While most of the world's top climbers waited patiently for the Karakoram to open, Chris Bonington started to file Trango Tower applications as regularly as his tax forms, beginning in 1972. In the spring of 1975 the coveted permission arrived, but just after similar tactics in Nepal had won him a crack at the Southwest Face of Everest for the fall of the same year. He contemplated trying both climbs, saying that "Everest is the cake, but Trango the icing." Reality forced a decision that a cake without icing was better than icing without cake. At the last minute he passed on his Trango permit to some friends who had an even more long-standing date with the Trangos. Joe Brown and Ian McNaught-Davis had first considered the climb while on Mustagh Tower together in 1956; nineteen years later, they were still eager to give it a try. The four other members of their team were Dave Potts, Martin Boysen, Will Barker, and Mo Anthoine. After the normal dose of 1975 porter delays, they reached the mountain in poor weather with very limited time. Difficult climbing up icy cracks brought them within 700 feet of the summit, where Martin Boysen had a climber's worst nightmare come true. His knee became stuck in a crack; the more he tried to free it the tighter it became wedged. Hours passed and his companions went down the fixed ropes to bring back bivouac gear so he could pass the night hanging by his leg at 20,000 feet. In desperation, Boysen hammered a knife-blade piton until it had a jagged edge, then used it to cut away the fabric from his thick wool pants, taking some flesh at the same time. Thus narrowed, his bloody knee slid out of the crack, and he slid down the ropes all the way to the base, where the team decided to abandon the effort.

Climbs of Nameless Tower, Paiyu Peak, and the Grand Cathedral in 1975 and 1976 barely scratched the surface of the area's potential. There were unexplored side valleys that could hide several Yosemites. Joe Brown came back from a walk up the Trango Glacier with the report that he had found "a whole series of Drus that looked as though they had been left there while their owner was deciding where to put them." Of the three main Trango Towers, only one had been climbed or attempted. The highest of all—the Great Trango Tower—rose above the rugged Dunge Glacier like the prow of a ship abandoned in the Polar Sea, its icy deck seven thousand feet above the surface of the frozen water.

11

To the Trango Towers

Our Trango Tower expedition celebrated the Fourth of July with fireworks and patriotic speeches at a barbecue. We had been invited to a party at the U.S. Embassy. We were surrounded by hundreds of people wearing that diverse mixture of bermuda shorts and business suits, halter tops and high fashion that sets American festivities apart from those of any other nation. Behind high walls in Islamabad, Pakistan, the scene had a movie-set unreality.

When the new U.S. ambassador spoke to the crowd, he said nothing about Independence Day we hadn't heard before, but a feeling of freedom welled up inside me. I looked at Kim and remembered a conversation at the last dinner of our Nun Kun expedition.

Maynard Cohick had been ecstatic over reaching the summit of Nun Kun; it had been a triumph of planning and hard work that he compared to other events in his life. He told Kim, who ski-bummed in the winters and guided in the summers, that he might find great happiness if he directed his life toward increased stability. Kim could well follow his own example toward a professional career, marriage, a family, and property. With this kind of security, Kim might feel more satisfied with life.

There was a pause and all eyes fell on Kim. He looked kindly at Maynard and replied, "Bullshit."

Everyone, including Maynard, had laughed heartily. The laughter not only recognized Kim's right to choose a free-form lifestyle but also recognized

The Great Trango Tower. Route ascends mixed rock and snow on left side of this face.

the conflicts in all lives that this group of climbers had only partially resolved by coming on the expedition. Few people—if any—could combine Maynard's success in professional life with Kim's life in the mountains. We all have to choose.

Climbers like Kim formed the core of our Trango expedition. We had a mountain guide, a free-lance writer, an unemployed geologist, and a carpenter. This foursome included Kim and me, John Roskelley, and Dennis Hennek. Each of us had at least a decade of hard climbing experience, two previous Himalayan expeditions, and two climbs on El Capitan. We were perfectly matched for an alpine-style technical climb in the Himalaya, but unable to pursue it without the help of more affluent people. Joining us were two climbing physicians, Jim Morrissey and Lou Buscaglia, who were paying more than their fair share to make our dreams come true. Morrissey was already somewhere on the Baltoro as doctor for a commercial trekking group. We were to meet him under the Trangos about July 14. Buscaglia was traveling with us.

In the morning our thoughts were on last-minute details before flying over the main crest of the Himalaya to the Skardu Valley in the Karakoram. The first hint that something was wrong came from the telephone. All circuits were jammed. The hotel manager informed us that the government had fallen. While we had been watching fireworks, a group of Pakistani generals had hatched a military coup. Prime Minister Bhutto was in custody and the country was under martial law.

The freedom we had just celebrated was suddenly very tenuous. I thought about Heinrich Harrer, who was imprisoned for years in India because World War II began while he was on an expedition to Nanga Parbat. But then we learned that the new government planned to honor the Bhutto regime's commitments. The only change was a sudden increase in the hat size of the army captain who had been appointed to accompany us to base camp. Captain Abdul Rashid took his job as liaison officer very seriously.

Just because our expedition was small and lightly equipped didn't mean we could escape government red tape. According to written policy, we had to procure such things as insurance for our porters and a list of gear for our liaison officer that would have enabled him to live comfortably at 28,000 feet, even though he was not going above the warm meadow at our 13,000-foot base camp. Unfortunately, the box containing most of his gear had been lost by one of the airlines en route. Although the gear was officially only on loan, it was usually donated, and liaison officers had come to expect about $1,500 of new equipment in addition to all food, expenses, and a per diem salary. We tried to persuade the captain that he would not need such things as expedition parkas and mountain boots.

Mr. Naseer Ullah Awan, the deputy minister of tourism, agreed that such equipment was not necessary for a Trango Tower liaison officer, but said that the regulations were made by the army and beyond his control. He helped us purchase the needed items from a returning Swiss trekking group. When we inquired about the porter situation he told us that recent expeditions had had no problems. Then he pulled out a handful of freshly printed booklets and made us the first to start a new tradition. Previously, porters had been hired on their good looks, a five-minute medical exam, and at best a note from another expedition. Now, each porter's service was to be recorded in a booklet that he would keep on his person. Expedition leaders would sign them, state time

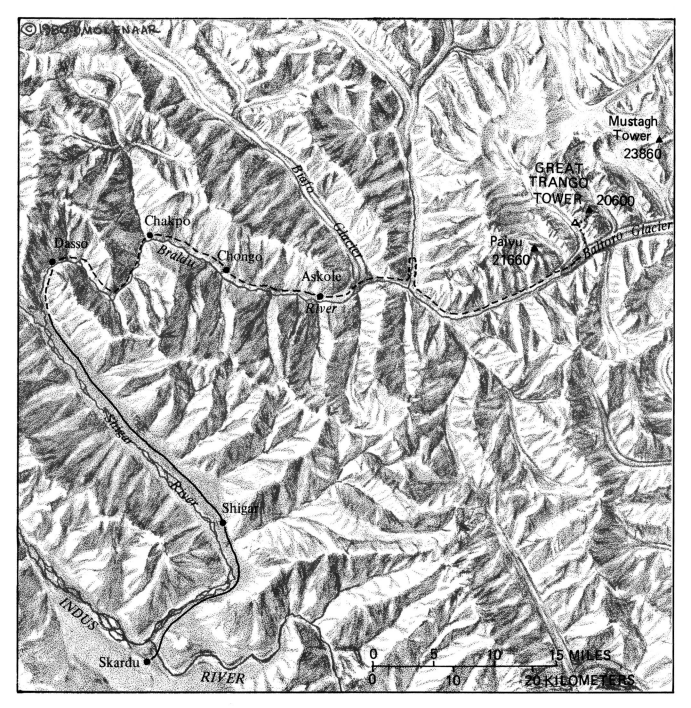

*Route to the
Trango
Towers*

served, and comment on how well the individual performed. Porters would have an inducement to keep their records clean, and within a few seasons expeditions would be able to hire porters with résumés and references.

To reach base camp we needed to fly to Skardu, drive forty-seven miles of jeep roads, then walk seventy more miles up the canyon of the Braldu River to the Baltoro Glacier. In 1975, I had made the same journey with the American K2 Expedition, with an extra thirty miles of glacier travel to reach that more distant peak. Beginning with 650 porters and nine climbers, the journey had taken seven weeks from our arrival in Islamabad. Now we were planning on seven *days* to base camp, with twenty porters.

Much of the time saved was the result of better flight and porter services, but by being able to move fast on the trail and the mountain we hoped to cut normal expedition land costs by more than half. Although porters were to be paid on the basis of set daily stages between certain campsites, there were hidden, time-dependent expenses. The quantity of both porter and climber food needing transport was proportional to the number of days in the mountains, and extra food meant extra porters—and more extra food for the extra porters to eat. Other expenses dependent on time were porter insurance, kerosene, and the liaison officer's insurance, food, and salary.

Our logistical plan was hardly original. On the afternoon in California when we used three hours and three notebook pages to lay our plans, we were seeking to emulate Eric Shipton. Shipton believed that "the only worthwhile expeditions were those that could be organized in half an hour on the back of an envelope." Our budget was $12,000, including air travel for three only, because the other three would already be in Asia. The K2 budget in 1975 had been $250,000.

We left Islamabad the morning of July 7, flying next to the ice tapestry of Nanga Parbat just before landing in the sandy desert of the Skardu Valley. Wind-sculpted dunes with treeless hillsides behind them brought back memories of Death Valley, which disappeared when our hired jeep took us into town. The valley's first impression of stillness was replaced by one of motion; people, horses, cattle, and military jeeps moved through the bustling bazaar under the rustling leaves of Lombardy poplars.

A dark figure, larger than the rest, shouted from the crowd and ran toward the jeep. I recognized Mohammed Hussain, a high-altitude porter with whom I had spent three months on K2 in 1975. He opened his arms with joy and we embraced like brothers. I told Dennis that this was the man who, in 1953, had carried frostbitten George Bell on his back for much of the distance from K2 to Skardu—over a hundred miles. In 1975, when Mohammed Hussain was a fifty-year-old veteran of twenty-five expeditions, I had seen him carry another sick man many miles across the Godwin-Austen Glacier. We hired him on the spot as the special porter required for our captain, who would also watch over base camp while we were on the peak. Mohammed's English was rusty from disuse, so we asked the captain to tell him in Urdu to be at our rest house at four the next morning to meet the jeeps.

After Mohammed took off at a trot toward his home seven miles up in the hills, the captain told us that we could never leave early in the morning because of the long list of supplies and formalities to attend to in Skardu. We explained that although it was his first visit to Skardu, we knew the town well and could pay baksheesh to get goods after store hours if the need arose. Unless we left well before dawn, glacier-fed streams from side valleys would rise so high during the heat of the day that the jeep couldn't pass. We hustled, accomplished everything and went to bed after midnight.

Our getaway in the jeeps went smoothly except for one great disappointment. Mohammed failed to show up. Our heavily laden vehicles took most of the day to reach the roadhead, forty-seven miles up the valley. The landscape was forever changing, beginning with a bridge over the broad Indus that led into a localized barrenness more devoid of life than the driest parts of our Southwest. Then the road would wind up to a pass, plunge through a grove of apricot trees into a village, and return to a world of rock, sand, and sage.

Near the confluence of the Shigar and Braldu rivers a long section of the road dipped into the flooding waters. We unloaded and walked an hour to Dasso, where we hired porters to bring our gear to the village for the night and to carry it for the next three days to Askole, the last village. There we planned to select a group of men who would double-stage to the mountain, moving the distance between two normal camps each day.

At five the next morning, while we were busy cooking breakfast and distributing loads to porters, an unexpected face showed up in the camp: Mohammed Hussain. What he had done was a new page for his legend.

When we had first met him on the street of Skardu, our captain had not properly translated our request for him to come at 4:00 A.M. Believing that we would never be ready to leave that early, he had told Mohammed not to come before ten. Mohammed had walked the seven miles from his home in Skardu with his personal gear only to find us gone. Undaunted, he started to walk. Continuing through the night without sleep, he caught us in Dasso—sixty miles from where he had started less than a day before!

We were about to begin twelve tortuous miles traversing canyon walls, one of the hardest stages of the approach. Mohammed made a special request to have a little lighter load than usual, emphasizing that he would carry his full share after he had rested. It was the least we could do, and we kept an extra porter for the day. Carrying just his personal gear, Mohammed set out after a cup of tea with some bounce in his step.

We stopped for the night in Chakpo, choosing for a camp a glade of fruit trees in which we had camped in 1975. Not a tree, a stone, or a doorway had changed. At first the constancy was gratifying; being there again brought back hundreds of little memories, otherwise lost forever. I could walk up a path and suddenly know exactly what was around the next bend.

Very quickly, however, Chakpo felt ominous. Time was standing still. I didn't like it, but I wasn't sure why. I sat down on my foam pad by a tree I'd rested under two years before, where I had photographed a deaf-mute spinning wool. That image had unusual meaning for me: it captured a haunting stare out of an ancient stillness—the essence of the Balti people's plight. As I lay thinking about that photograph, the same deaf-mute, wearing the same tattered rags, sat down in the same place and began spinning wool! I took another, almost identical photograph. As I walked through each successive village, my thoughts wavered from the medieval scenes before my eyes, to flashes of memory, to the 1977 date on my diary page. My identity in the present weakened, and I ended the day's entry with: "I feel as if I had been reincarnated!"

In Chongo a voice from a courtyard called, "Galen Sahib! Galen Sahib!" I recognized Ali, the porter who had carried my personal gear through these same villages toward K2. He hugged me in the Islamic way, first one shoulder, then the other, forgetting that I might not be overjoyed at the sight of a man I had last seen walking away from Urdukas with 250 other strikers when the first snow fell. He continued to tell me in broken English the whereabouts of each of our 1975 high-altitude porters. Most were on big expeditions.

I walked on through my fondest dream of 1975: to be traveling the same route with a small expedition of friends moving with great efficiency and happiness. We stopped for photographs, soaked in hot springs, and ended each day with relaxed joy.

Askole was the last village, positioned spectacularly on a shelf that jutted out from the canyon wall. Above, vertical cliffs of white granitic rock rose against the blue sky. Below, the almost constant whitewater of the Braldu River overwhelmed the jade hue of the glacial stream. From across the valley the shelf appeared level enough to have been bulldozed—as indeed it had, by an advance of the Baltoro Glacier.

The Balti people live in a backwater of civilization, where only the barest outlines of the past are known. They have no written history—in fact, no written language at all. Their dialect is related to ancient Tibetan, but too distant from any present language to be understood by even neighboring peoples. Anthropologists in search of the Baltis' origin have traveled so many blind alleys that serious consideration is being given to a recent proposal to drill through the thousand-odd feet of ice of the Baltoro Glacier in search of artifacts that may have been buried by the advancing ice.

In Askole we asked for porters who would make the normal four-day carry to the Baltoro Glacier in two days. We offered double pay (the same net cost for us), quality food, and a substantial list of gratuities such as wool socks and sunglasses. To our surprise, many of the porters who had come from Dasso were interested. We had wanted to use Askole men as much as possible because they were reputed to be the toughest. Thirty-five Askole men showed up bearing postcards from the 1975 K2 expedition with the notation that the bearer was among the faithful 57 out of 650 who stuck with that expedition all the way to base camp. Unfortunately, the cards had not stuck with their owners; many of the men I had never seen before. We kept eight Dasso porters and hired twelve Askole men.

Their final demand was for fresh meat to eat along the trail. I had an idea that would help them keep their promise to make the trip in two days. We would buy Askole's largest goat for the exorbitant price of 600 rupees (sixty dollars), and march it on a leash for two days. If we camped at the toe of the Baltoro the second night, the porters and the sahibs would celebrate and eat the goat together. If, however, we camped short of the glacier, the climbers alone would eat it.

The offer was instantly accepted, and the game was on. At four the next morning we were up, breaking camp into porter loads and getting ready to move before the heat of the day. A few stars still shone in the clear sky. The early morning was warm and dry, with no sound of machines, only the comforting roar of the Braldu in flood, birds chirping, and people murmuring.

In Askole I did not sense the timelessness that had rushed over me in Chakpo. Tennis shoes supplied by expeditions had become more common than goatskin mukluks. Digital wristwatches were replacing coral and turquoise as

Right
John Roskelley carrying a live goat across a bridge made from willow twigs, Karakoram
Far right
Mohammed Hussain, who walked sixty miles in a day to work for the expedition.

symbols of prosperity. And the Lambardar, Askole's feudal lord and mayor, had improved on traditional Askole decor by refurbishing his dining room with a Persian carpet and an American aluminum-and-polypropylene lawn chair from our 1975 K2 expedition.

At the end of the first day we came to a frail bridge of woven willow twigs draped across a raging torrent. Several strands broke after only seven porters had crossed. The porters solemnly announced that the goat would have to be slaughtered on the spot. I argued that they knew the condition of the bridge when they made the deal, and it was their duty to bring the goat across. The impasse was broken when John Roskelley shouldered the goat, tied it to his own back, and carried it over. The porters cheered and treated us with a closeness I had never known on my former journey.

The next day's travel brought us to Paiyu camp at the toe of the Baltoro. Several weeks of clear weather had created a haze that made the mountains much less distinct. In 1975, storms had kept us in whiteouts for days, but in-between were crystalline visions of the mountains—ideal for photography. Now the Great Trango Tower poked its summit above a foreground ridge in the muted tones of Yosemite on a summer afternoon.

Paiyu camp was in the only grove of trees in hundreds of square miles. Cottonwoods followed a spring-fed stream down a hillside, flanked by willows, wild roses, and finally the sagebrush and ephedra through which we had walked the entire way. There, camped in a clearing, was Jim Morrissey. He had waited less than a day for us: incredible luck in synchronizing two uncertain itineraries.

I was as transfixed by the change in Morrissey as by the lack of change elsewhere in the Karakoram. The last time I had seen the forty-one-year-old heart surgeon, he had been departing from a restaurant in Pavlovian response to his beeper, the bounce in his step matched by that of his stomach. His eyes had had the flash of an Irish youth, but the overall impression was one of an athlete beyond his prime. Now those same eyes gazed from the body of a mountain man, at least twenty pounds lighter and infinitely tougher than the out-of-shape physician I had seen in Stockton. He was excited about a route he had seen on the southwest face of the tower, one that he thought all of us could attempt together.

That evening—only our second since Askole—the porters feasted on fresh goat meat, leaving only small amounts for us sahibs. We reveled in the success of our approach plans, which had saved us several extra loads of porter and climber food. Lou Buscaglia, however, was having trouble with the pace. He showed up later, feet blistered, tired, and depressed.

In the morning we walked onto the rock-covered glacier, relatively unconcerned about finding a route over what appeared to be continuously easy but tedious terrain. We came upon an area of exposed ice with raging torrents and high walls that we could have easily skirted with boots and crampons. However, we were wearing running shoes and shorts. Although we could have unpacked and changed, we had to lead the way for porters, also in tennis shoes, so we chose a route that headed for a sandy gully on the opposite side of the glacier, rather than a more direct diagonal over ice to the Trango Tower.

The gully was a gentle paradise set between steep hillsides and the great lateral moraines of the Baltoro. There we found wildflowers in profusion, weathered junipers, and the fresh tracks of ibex, mountain sheep, brown bear, fox, and snow leopard. We turned left alongside the Trango Glacier until we were opposite the Great Trango Tower. A wide spot in the gully offered a perfect site for base camp. A stream meandered from the ice, laced with familiar fireweed, monkshood, and cinquefoil that decorate landscapes throughout the circumpolar realm of the alpine life zone. Large boulders lay widely separated on the gravel, perfect for practice climbing while we spent a few days acclimatizing and studying the route.

That evening we celebrated our good fortune. We had made the fastest expedition approach march to the Baltoro in history. All of us were healthy, and our proposed route looked quite feasible. The weather had been clear for a month, making it the best Karakoram climbing season in forty years.

In camp, Jim Morrissey handed me a package from my lady Jo Sanders in California. She had sent a Beethoven tee shirt and her results of throwing the *I Ching* for us. The tee shirt had a special meaning, because she knew that my first clear view of the Trango Towers had come after days of storm in 1975 when I awoke to the sounds of a Beethoven concerto on a tape deck, as the sun's first rays struck the peaks.

The quotes from the *I Ching* were quite another matter. I would not normally find guidance in ancient phrases written by an unknown Chinese, phrases located now by Jo's throwing coins in America. The *I Ching* was just a big fortune cookie, filled with obscure references that could apply to anyone. That was my opinion until I looked carefully at the quotes.

The first was a hexagram titled "Waiting." It told of "clouds in the heavens" and how all beings have need of nourishment from above. It advised the reader thus:

"Strength in the face of danger grows agitated and has not the patience to wait." It concluded, "We should not worry and seek to shape the future by interfering in things before the time is ripe. We should quietly fortify the body with food and drink and the mind with gladness and good cheer. Fate comes when it will, and thus we are ready."

I looked into the cloudless sky, and thought of our plans for a fast alpine-style climb. There seemed to be no message here.

The other hexagram was called "Obstruction." It had the dual element of a mountain and water, and it went further to describe "a steep inaccessible mountain" with "obstructions that appear in the course of time but that can and should be overcome." Then came a translation of the judgment to be followed:

"OBSTRUCTION. The southwest furthers. The northeast does not further. It furthers one to see the great man. Perseverance brings good fortune."

I looked at the Great Trango and wondered at the coincidence that the route we were planning began on the southwest side, whereas we had first considered going from the Dunge Glacier due northeast of the peak. On the upper part of the mountain, however, we still planned to follow the great east face, and I hoped that none of us would "see the great man," realizing in that moment that I was giving serious consideration to these ancient words.

After the porters were paid off we went to sleep under a clear sky. At one in the morning we were awakened by rain. I thought first of the *I Ching* message, and then of the classic date for the end of stable weather in the Karakoram each summer: July 15. Even though this date was derived from a historian's over-precise rendering of various opinions that the weather turned

bad about the middle of July, I wondered: the first raindrops were falling within the first hour after midnight on the fifteenth. I was to keep wondering as the rain continued for five long days.

On the second night of the storm, torrential rains filled every watercourse. House-sized boulders plunged down the gully behind us, creating sparks that left the wet air scented with ozone. The sound would begin with a low rumble, rise to a great clashing, then wane just as we began to rise from our sleeping bags. Once, the noise came far too close, and the four of us leapt for the tent door at the same instant, only to wedge to a stop together, like a child's hand filled with cookies in the neck of a jar. John, whose tent had been hit by an avalanche in the Pamirs, spent the rest of the night with his boots on.

Unknown to us, Chris Bonington and Doug Scott were fighting for their lives only twenty miles away on the Ogre, a 23,900-foot granite peak of much the same technical difficulty as the Trangos. Bonington later called the storm the worst he had ever experienced in the mountains. Had our own approach march been any more efficient, without the delays of lost baggage and red tape in Islamabad, we, too, would have been on our mountain.

Once, when the clouds lifted briefly, the Trango Towers appeared veiled in white, totally out of condition for climbing. Avalanches and rockfalls boomed down the gully we planned to ascend. I had no fixation that we had to reach the summit: I was happy just to be back in the Karakoram. I wrote in my diary, "So here we are, ground to a halt by the first poor weather in more than a month. But it is such a wild, pleasant place that I feel little frustration. I do fear that the weather may defeat us, but I can accept that. 'Waiting' in the *I Ching* has much more meaning now."

Upper left
Trango Towers,
Karakoram Himalaya
Left
Hanging village in the
canyon of the Braldu,
Karakoram

12 | Shangri-La

Two classics of Himalayan literature share almost no common ground. *The Conquest of Everest*, by Sir John Hunt, is a factual account of men who gave their all to win the earth's highest mountain. *Shangri-La*, by James Hilton, is a novel that stretches the quiet beauty, ordered lives, giant landscapes, and fabled longevity of mountain peoples into a fantasy of immortality.

Visitors to the Himalaya hope to leave Hunt's world of striving and become immersed in Hilton's world of simple living and serenity. For days, weeks, or even months they relish the experience of visiting remote villages like Askole, at first unaware of their addiction to things that are missing. Askole's lack of written language, plumbing, doctors, and games of skill eventually gnaws at them. To introduce these things would surely destroy the very quality of timelessness that they treasure.

There is indeed a hint of immortality in high Himalayan villages, but it comes from a continuity of ritual, rather than an imperishability of individual lives. We make a mistake if we think that merely by being in a place we can put on, like a coat, the way of life there. We seem to hope that a night course in Zen and an air ticket to Asia will somehow put us in touch with the earth again.

The visits of expeditions reflect the inevitable real-life conflict between characters out of *The Conquest of Everest* and *Shangri-La*. Concern about the

Afternoon light in the Braldu Gorge, Karakoram

conflict is not something hooked to the coattails of the recent environmental movement, but a matter of long-standing debate among mountaineers. In 1943, before Everest was climbed or *Shangri-La* written, Eric Shipton wrote, "Many of the expeditions—Italian, German, French, international—which followed the early attempts to climb Everest, were run with an extravagance which made the Everest expeditions seem modest by comparison. Fantastic equipment was evolved, dynamite brought to blow away obstacles, aeroplanes used for dumping supplies on the mountain, all the delicacies known to the culinary art were provided to sustain exhausted climbers, whole populations were uprooted from their homes to carry this stuff up the glaciers—with the consequent risk of famine the following year due to the neglect of agriculture." Shipton also described how disruption of the normal life of the country was "one of the principal objections of the Tibetan officials to Everest expeditions." Mount Everest remained closed to outsiders for many years because of these disruptions.

Although large-scale endeavors in the Himalaya dated back to the nineteenth century, before 1950 not a single one had ever succeeded in achieving its purpose. Returnees from these failures were welcomed home as heroes; their efforts were considered triumphs of the spirit. The media remained oblivious to the simple fact that the succession of highest summits ever climbed had been entirely the province of light expeditions. After 1950, however, this tradition was overwhelmed. Between 1953 and 1956, eight of the dozen highest peaks in the world were climbed for the first time by great expeditions. Only one of the big dozen—26,750-foot Cho Oyu—was climbed by a light party, but this climb by Herbert Tichy's three-man expedition in 1954 was all but forgotten in the wake of Everest publicity.

The use of oxygen became standard for 8,000-meter peaks. In the thirties, Frank Smythe, who had reached 28,000 feet without it, wrote, "To climb breathing oxygen, in order to reach a summit, would be a dreadful anticlimax to the work of an expedition; it would, indeed, be in the nature of an insult to that work. If the mountain is climbed thus, the ascent will not be a genuine one from a mountaineering standpoint, and the mountain will still await a mountaineer who can, by his own unaided powers, overcome the problem set by Nature."

After the successful ascent of Everest with oxygen, *The Conquest of Everest* reported in an appendix by team members Pugh and Ward: "The futile controversy over the ethics of using oxygen, and the failure to accept the findings of pioneers in its application, handicapped for thirty years the introduction of a method which promises to revolutionize high-altitude mountaineering. Apart from the question of whether mountains over 27,000 feet can be climbed without its use, oxygen undoubtedly reduces the mountaineering hazards and greatly increases subjective appreciation of the surroundings, which, after all, is one of the chief reasons for climbing."

Some mountaineers predicted that interest in Everest would greatly decline after it was finally climbed. A few news reporters even predicted the end of the sport, since no higher achievement was possible.

Everest, however, remained a supreme goal, and the style in which it had been climbed continued to influence expeditions from all over the world. The 1963 American Everest Expedition was modeled after the 1953 success. Planning for the 1975 American K2 Expedition was strongly based on that of Everest in 1963; the leader, Jim Whittaker, was chosen by the prospective climbers, who thought his ascent of Everest in the past would draw funding and help procure permission for the peak.

Mount Everest swallows the mountaineering records of most of its climbers. Experienced Englishmen who visited the mountain on early expeditions were forever after called "Everesters." Edmund Hillary suffered especially in this regard, since he became identified with large expeditionary tactics that he had never favored. His original involvement with Everest was through Shipton's reconnaissance and plan for a lightweight climb. He was a member of a Shipton "jaunt" through eastern Nepal during which two dozen peaks over 20,000 feet were climbed for the first time. His one big expedition to Everest had included ten climbers and twenty-seven Sherpas.

By contrast, an Italian effort in 1973 utilized 64 climbers and 120 Sherpas. The team arrived in five Italian Air Force Hercules C-130s, and brought their own helicopter with four pilots and six mechanics. Although the Nepalese Foreign Ministry expressly prohibited the use of the helicopter above base camp except for medical emergencies, it made two flights a week into the Western Cwm at 21,000 feet, thus bypassing the Khumbu icefall—the most difficult and dangerous part of the climb. Fresh vegetables, meat, booze, and new personnel were taken up, while potential summit climbers were flown down to Lukla at 9,000 feet for a complete rest before going high again.

In base camp, each two climbers lived in a six-man tent equipped with propane lighting and kerosene heating. Count Monzino lived in a tent-palace that had wall-to-wall carpets, a sitting room, dining room, bedroom, shower, Porta-Potty, bar, and a huge oak desk with a leather top and brass studs. While visiting, Hillary saw a most substantial stash of canned spaghetti, bologna, peaches, Coca-Cola, and beer. Five radio technicians kept contact with the outside world by a sideband hook-up to Kathmandu, where a teletype and a radio shack at the airport were manned eighteen hours a day. When the helicopter crashed in the Western Cwm, they simply radioed to Italy for another one, which was promptly delivered. The wreck was left in the snows, where it gradually merged with the ice and began to move down the Khumbu Icefall. Scientists predict that it will emerge from the toe of the glacier sometime in the early 1980s.

Expeditions customarily paid bonuses to Sherpas who carried to the highest camps. In the fifties these were on the order of an extra day's wage for a carry to the South Col—perhaps thirty rupees at best. The Italians paid 150 rupees for each carry to the Col, and 1,000 rupees for a carry to the highest camp. In this manner, they secured a comfortable base of supplies at over 27,000 feet, and guaranteed that less affluent expeditions in the future would not be able to satisfy their Sherpas with anywhere near the same payment.

For an expenditure of well over a million dollars, five Italians and three Nepalese had repeated Hillary's 1953 route.

Hillary came back from the Italian Base camp, which he had visited while building a school in the Khumbu for Sherpa children, and was interviewed by the press. "What Senor Monzino has shown," he said, "is that if you have a couple of platoons of alpine troops, which is what he has, and a couple of helicopters, which is what he has, and unlimited equipment and funds, which he also has, then the climbing of the South Col route is a relatively straightforward procedure. We shouldn't regard this as a mountaineering expedition. What it is is taking a group of service people and getting them to work together

Above
Porters on the way to K2
Upper right
*An Askole porter with clothes from Europe,
shoes from Japan, and an
American cigarette.*
Right
*Balti father and son in Askole.
Note undyed woolens and handmade toy.*

on a difficult and challenging objective. It is more of a training program. As a mountaineer, I think he would have been better carrying it out in the European Alps. It has been a very competent military operation, but it has nothing to do with mountaineering. I hope in the future that Everest will be left to mountaineering parties composed of small groups of enthusiastic climbers. It has reached the height of the ridiculous."

*Cloud halo over
Dobani, Karakoram*

Hillary, however, was no longer just a mountaineer speaking for himself. Big expedition machinery reached to very high levels. A few days after his interview, the Italian Embassy in Kathmandu asked the British Embassy to ask Hillary if he wished to correct or modify his statement. Hillary wrote to Monzino:

"I certainly have no desire to cast any reflection on the leadership and organization of your party or on the courage, competency, and determination of your young men. In fact, the contrary was my intention. I felt that your party was so strong and well organized that the final result was almost inevitable, as much as anything can be inevitable on a mountain like Everest. As a traditionalist in mountaineering matters, it would be hypocrisy to suggest that I am a supporter of massive expeditions, however successful they may be. Big expeditions have been a growing trend in the Himalaya over the past decade. Perhaps I am old-fashioned in wishing to see a return to the smaller, less professional type of operation."

How different the history of high-altitude mountaineering might have been had Hillary summitted with Shipton's proposed small team without oxygen. Shipton, however, when asked shortly before his death what he would do differently if he had his life to live over again, said, "I wouldn't have spent so much time mucking about Mount Everest. I would have gone to more peaks under 25,000 feet that could be climbed with a few classic tools by a few friends."

Like Shipton, every mountaineer who goes to the Himalaya is confronted by the dilemma posed at the beginning of this chapter: that of trying to find something of *Shangri-La* while living in the heritage of the *Conquest of Everest*.

In the almost thirty years since the first climb of Everest, the rivulet of visitors has become a destructive torrent, fed by an ever-growing number of new streams. As recently as 1966, forty-four percent of all tourists entering Nepal were from the United States. By 1978, almost eighty-five percent were from other nations. American climbers had lost their ability to influence the Himalaya's future. Forty-seven expeditions went to Nepal in 1978, up from nineteen the year before. Trekking likewise increased eleven percent in 1978, and increased another thirty-six percent in the first half of 1979.

As mountain tourism becomes a full-fledged industry with few international restraints, the fragile ecosystems and ancient ways of life in the Himalaya are odds-on losers in a multinational competition for momentary material advantage.

13 | Shipton's Dream

For the first time in four days, the rain stopped. The lifting clouds exposed a grim sight. The Trango Towers, far above the snowline at 16,000 feet, looked like the wildest peaks of Patagonia after an ice storm. Sudden warmth from the sun was causing avalanches to sweep every face of every tower. In the couloir where we planned to begin our climb, snow slides were setting in motion great boulders that caromed downward for thousands of feet, rearranging the topography several times in an hour.

I headed toward the Baltoro Glacier with a pack of camera equipment, hoping that a look at the higher peaks would give me a better idea about the weather. The rough trail went along a sandy hillside that smelled of wet sage, reminding me of other times after thunderstorms on the east side of the Sierra Nevada. Wildflowers and rivulets of rainwater reinforced the image. Then a fresh mark brought me to attention. A cat track as big as my fist was perfectly imprinted in the wet glacial silt. It was unmarked by raindrops, less than a half hour old. I dropped all other thoughts and endeavors to enter the snow leopard's world and follow its sign. Leaving behind all but a camera and 500-mm lens, I padded up the hill, following its tracks as the cat must have followed the ibex, whose tracks were now mingled with its own.

The ibex trail angled up the hillside, following a track worn by the passage of its ancestors. In the center of a bed of old tracks, nearly erased, were sharp hoof cuts in the soil and the soft, broad pad marks of the leopard. Near the edge of a ravine both sets of tracks turned abruptly up the hillside. I followed them to a point where they diverged; the ibex continued up, but the leopard veered into the ravine. I followed the leopard tracks, but only for a few feet, since the ravine

Paiyu Peak from the summit ridge of Great Trango Tower

was cut into morainal mud and boulders, and the overhanging walls were forty feet high. Without a rope I couldn't descend where the tracks disappeared. I walked back and forth, searching for a place to cross, and found none. The ravine appeared to have been deepened, or perhaps even created, by the recent storm.

I had the feeling that I was being watched. The leopard may have seen me while tracking the ibex, and dodged into the ravine where it could hide under the overhangs. I sat down on a boulder and looked for movement. There was none. Less than a mile from our base camp, I was in paradise, even if the leopard never showed itself. Clouds were lifting from the higher peaks, exposing Concordia and the Gasherbrum peaks in the sunset light. The pursuit of the leopard had temporarily locked me into the present where I entered a state of optimistic expectation about my involvement with the natural world.

I realized that my paradise was not accessible to everyone. A survivor of a plane crash, sitting on the same boulder, would feel oppressed by the remoteness and want nothing more than to be back in civilization immediately. A trekker with porters and guides would never find my solitude. I returned to base camp without seeing the snow leopard, but with an even more fulfilling vision.

The next morning we were up and packing by 4:30; by 7:00 we were on the opposite side of the glacier, sorting through ropes and food we had cached on our first day. Our chosen couloir would have been a deathtrap for a normal, siege-style expedition, faced with the task of climbing it several times with heavy loads to stock fixed camps. We planned one trip.

The odds were with us in the cool of the morning before the sun unfroze the latch on untold tons of poised rock and snow, ready to explode down the couloir. With sixty-pound loads we forced our bodies upward as hard as they would go, walking up steep, loose boulders and cramponing on frozen avalanche debris. Like snails on a city sidewalk, we inched along with our homes on our backs in the presence of forces that could squash us without warning.

Kim, John, Dennis, and I reached the 17,000-foot col within minutes of one another; we were the best-matched foursome I'd ever climbed with. The 3,500 vertical feet with heavy loads at altitude had taken less than four hours at a pace accelerated by fear of the rising sun. The col was a haven of almost-level granite terraces decorated with red primroses and green mosses. We were face-to-face with Uli Biaho Tower and Paiyu Peak across the gorge. We busied ourselves moving rocks to make a tent platform.

At two in the afternoon, a tremendous avalanche roared 6,000 feet down the face of the Great Trango, missed our protected col, and swept the couloir clean. We yelled. No answer. A fresh tongue of sickening white snow curved out of sight, trackless and empty as our hearts.

No one discussed descending. We intuitively followed the "Aleister Crowley rescue principle," derived from a 1905 Kanchenjunga expedition. Crowley was ostracized for continuing afternoon tea while his companions were buried in an avalanche. He said that he had warned them not to be on the slope after midday; if they were in trouble, he wasn't about to risk his life for those already dead.

But Jim and Lou had done nothing wrong. They had only been pursuing the desire we all had to climb the tower. Indeed, Jim Morrissey was acting selflessly; he had stayed back to help Lou.

The upper ice field on Great Trango Tower

We lingered there for hours, fearing that we had lost our friends but not daring to descend for a look until the evening chill firmed the upper mountain once again. The sound of distant voices in the couloir affected me as if the world's heaviest pack had been lifted from my shoulders. Knowing that they were alive and well was only part of the story, however. We had a long discussion about whether they should continue. There was no way we could climb the tower alpine-style with our limited supplies if, as in the couloir, our climbing time was more than doubled. Our very safety rested in speed and light weight.

Lou had already hinted that he would stop at the col if he found the going too rough. Jim was another matter, although John was adamant that Jim be allowed to make his own decision. He talked of his great personal debt to Jim for introducing him to the Himalaya in 1973, where he reached the 26,795-foot top of Dhaulagiri. All of us owed Jim a debt for making the present expedition possible. Even so, I questioned whether the four of us who had had far more experience on technical terrain didn't owe him the benefit of our caution. Of all of us, Jim seemed the most confident about the ease of climbing the tower. He had considered soloing the Great Trango if we didn't show up; this was something I would not have done myself. John said that Jim could simply jumar with mechanical ascenders on the rope after we led the way. I was concerned with more than safety, happiness, and success. If we got into trouble through storm or accident, Jim would be in the worst position because he would have the greatest difficulty extricating himself.

When Jim and Lou came in sight, we climbed down to help them over the last steep part where it was necessary to traverse a nearly vertical cliff. They were greatly relieved to be at the col, and they related a spine-chilling tale.

In the middle of the couloir, Lou had commented on a pretty waterfall. Jim realized it was not a waterfall, but an avalanche. Only seconds before it swept through the couloir like a tidal wave, they both scrambled up the sidewall, barely out of reach.

Fatigued and blistered, Lou decided to camp at the col until we came down from the climb. Jim wanted to go on. After dinner, John began to talk about it. Jim was surprised that anyone questioned his place on the summit team. He obviously trusted all of us and he said he knew what he was getting into. Although he lacked our background on big rock climbs, he was a fit, experienced mountaineer. He offered to rappel back to the col if the climbing proved too difficult for him. None of us could deny a place in the party to a healthy member who had made the whole enterprise possible, and we admired Jim's guts.

Evening at the col was clear and still. We were far above the Baltoro Glacier near six of the seventeen highest peaks in the world; a small circle of friends in the midst of giants. Hidden Peak and Gasherbrum IV pierced the horizon above the sweeping curves of the Baltoro, but we were still too low to see the other big peaks, which were blocked by the Grand Cathedral and the first Trango.

We said goodbye to Lou before dawn and shouldered packs that looked disturbingly small and felt disturbingly heavy. Kim and I had somewhat lighter loads because we were to be leaders for the day. We would alternate pitches and fix ropes for the others. They would follow on Jumar mechanical ascenders, pull out the ropes, and bring them up to us so that we could continue leading.

Sunrise caught Kim leading an ice-filled crack in the best alpine granite we had ever seen. He moved with slow grace and confidence, belying the effort he was expending to climb a crack in double boots at 18,000 feet. We were in ecstasy; the weather, the rock, the surroundings, and the companionship were all as fine as we could ever desire. When I reached Kim in the middle of the headwall, we looked at each other and giggled with delight.

On my next lead I had the choice of beginning a long rock section that would consume most of the day, or veering left up a steep ramp of snow and ice. The headwall offered greater immediate safety, but at the expense of a long-range threat; if the weather didn't hold I knew from 1975 that our fine pink granite could disappear under a crust of ice during a storm. The best we could hope for was a four- or five-day clear spell, and we might need all of that time to complete the climb. I chose the snow ramp, gambling on passing the chute that had spilled yesterday's monster avalanche before the morning thaw, and also knowing that the earlier avalanche had taken away much of the potential for an avalanche now.

For a tense two hours we pitted our speed against the rising sun. Then we gained the ridge crest and ate lunch below a long icefield covered with a thin layer of snow that was the source of the avalanches we had witnessed. We chose what appeared to be a 500-foot beeline to a giant ledge up an area where the surface snow had already slid. The distance proved to be 1,500 feet and the ledge was nonexistent. We found only a narrow, corniced crest overhanging a 6,000-foot drop to the Dunge Glacier. It was separated from the main wall by a wide gap.

There was no natural bivouac site in the area, so we dug a tiny platform into the cornice. Just under the snow was blue ice that took hours to chop away with our axes. We had no tent, so we tied ourselves to a safety rope anchored to ice screws and scrunched together on Ensolite pads.

Dinner was a disappointment. We discovered that we had left much of our food at the col. The single stove refused to work properly and it took an hour to warm a pot of water. After a meager meal we counted what was left for two more days of climbing: three packets of hot chocolate, six tea bags, one packet of soup, a half pound of cheese, and two bacon bars. No one complained, even though the lack of food was due to an oversight; we had always planned to go as light as possible high on the peak. We watched the last light move up the faces of Masherbrum, Chogolisa, the four Gasherbrums, Broad Peak, and K2.

We awoke at our 19,000-foot bivouac while stars were still shining and the snowy landscape was locked in the phosphorescent blue of night. As we packed for the push to the summit, we were treated to a light show. Shadows of the highest peaks were cast into the stratosphere against the purple predawn sky.

Before the sun hit the peaks we rappelled down to the icefield, leaving our bivouac gear on the platform. A 500-foot traverse across the top of the icefield placed us left of the cleft that had separated our bivouac from the main wall. It was Dennis and John's day to lead, and they chose a deep rock chimney filled with ice. Wearing crampons to climb thin ice over rock, they spent seven hours gaining six hundred feet, marveling about the fine quality of the rock and the interesting nature of the climbing. It was as if a classic route in Yosemite had been elevated to twenty thousand feet, coated in ice, and presented to us as a new challenge.

Overleaf
Kim Schmitz climbing 5.8 in double boots at 18,000 feet on Great Trango Tower. Baltoro Glacier, Grand Cathedral, and Hidden Peak in the background.

While Dennis and John alternated leads, Kim, Jim and I hung from pitons for long hours, separated in our positions and our thoughts. Without bivouac gear or food to haul on this summit day, we had nothing to do while the others labored. I found it very relaxing to let my mind follow random pathways, influenced by sights and sounds around me rather than by the forced awareness of the act of climbing.

I saw Kim profiled against the sky in what would have been a heroic pose, except that his chin was touching his chest, his eyes were closed, and his expression was that of a sleeping child. I wanted to take a photograph, but I knew that an exposure that would catch his shadowed face would change the sky and rock surrounding him to tones of burned-out white. I fiddled with my camera, then took it from my neck and clipped it to a carabiner in front of me. To my horror I watched the strap zip across the metal and disappear, with the camera, into space. One end of the new "backpacker's camera strap" that a company had given me to test had unclipped itself from the camera body. Somewhere, six thousand feet below, fragments of metal and glass joined the debris of the Trango Glacier.

At first I was angry with myself for losing the camera, and with it the opportunity to record the details of the climb. Then I felt a freedom from the device and a rush of appreciation for my own eyesight and memory. Every hour or so we moved up to new positions in the chimney, made ourselves comfortable, and renewed our musings.

In the middle of the afternoon John and Dennis reached an ice ramp at the top of the chimney. As I jumared up to a ledge, Dennis led toward an awesome cornice on the summit ridge only two hundred feet above. We began to worry about time; in order to return to the bivouac by dark, we would soon have to turn around whether we had made the summit or not.

Dennis found an easy notch hidden at the edge of the cornice, and soon all five of us were walking along the narrow crest toward the highest point. We were surrounded by icy mountains in late afternoon light, all in familiar positions save one. Nameless Tower, marked on maps as the highest of the Trangos, was already below us before we made the final rise to the summit. Surveyors nearly half a century before had measured the highest point of the Great Trango that was visible from the foot of the Baltoro Glacier—a rock crest several hundred feet lower than the true summit. Only as we neared the summit, however, did we know for certain that we were climbing the highest of the Trango Towers for the first time. Reinhold Messner's intuitive name for our peak, "The Great Trango Tower," had proven correct.

On top, we hugged each other with joy. The air was so still we stripped off jackets and gloves to pose in tee shirts for photos. We were in the center of the universe, perched on a cloud above a dream world of peaks and glaciers. I wanted to roll in the snow and laugh, but I knew we were not home free. The prospect of the descent weighed heavily in all of our minds.

I borrowed Dennis's camera, loaded it with my film, and put seventy-two pictures through it in minutes. I wished I had had endless film and endless hours to use it. We spent only thirty minutes on top, taking photographs and just gazing at the powerful land masses above and below. Masherbrum was the closest giant, dominating the southern sky like the cathedral of a medieval town. In the distance a line of even higher summits traced the Chinese border from Hidden Peak to K2. Beyond, dust from the deserts of Sinkiang rode the winds. The boldest vision, however, was not the distant sights, but the forest of granite peaks surrounding us, all but a few unvisited, unclimbed. Some, like Paiyu, Uli Biaho, and the Ogre, had names known to mountaineers, but most were unknown, unnamed points on the map. Here was the land of my dreams, where granite walls like those of my home Sierra Nevada rose far larger and far higher in a remote corner of the world.

Going down meant rappels, interminable rappels, set up by two men, descended by five, retrieved by two, and then set by the first two again. Night caught us on the icefield traverse after one of our ropes had been left behind on a jammed rappel. We tied the other three ropes together in the gathering darkness and fixed them to ice screws. We had only a few feet to spare when we got to the bivouac platform at ten o'clock.

We awoke to see K2 piercing the rays of the sun in the eastern sky, Broad Peak flushed in gold, and Masherbrum gilded along its north prow. Rappels on ice screws and pickets brought us down the ice face; many more on rock pitons took us to the col, where Lou congratulated us and we packed for the final dash down the gully to the glacier.

At base camp, Mohammed Hussain greeted us with open arms and we renewed our contact with the basics of living. After only four days up and down the face, small things took on an intensified importance. We reveled in level ground, flowers, running water, and most of all in food. We prepared our victory dinner of shrimp cocktail, hot tea, mashed potatoes with butter and chives, fried beef patties, rose cabernet wine, cognac, and blueberry pie.

We sat up in the starlight, talking and looking about in wonder—a communion of souls. The world glowed with the richness of the last days.

The march out began like a fairytale. Two ibex appeared on the ridge above camp in the early morning and whistled an eerie tone before turning away. Near the toe of the glacier a band of about thirty urial mountain sheep—relatives of our bighorn—moved noiselessly over the rocky hillsides at full speed with heads lilting in a single plane like a flight of birds. We reached Paiyu in the evening and looked back to see a storm move in over the Baltoro. We had finished the climb with less than a day to spare. The once golden granite of our Trango was now as gray as the sky, as dark as the shadows, and as dim as the dusty air.

After dinner I sat on a boulder and wrote in my diary:

This land is mine because we succeeded; I know it is an illusion, but it makes each footstep a pleasure, a return to life and love through a known channel. A rock here, a familiar tree, a cliff profile are now personal things as set in my mind as the position of the bathroom light switch in the dark. Now the clouds have lowered on the Trangos. Snow must be falling and Paiyu is so safe, so comfortable. The trees are alive in the wind and raindrops just hit this page.

At the decadent hour of seven, I crawled out of the tent—the first time since Islamabad I had slept past five in the morning. I walked around Paiyu, seeing in the harsh light what looked like a war zone in place of the wonder of the night before. Bunkers had been dug into the hillsides by armies of porters. Trees were stripped as surely as by shrapnel. Worst of all was the place we called the Battlefield of Turds, where the 1977 Japanese K2 Expedition had camped. The earth seemed to bear yet the warmth of the passage of their 950 porters;

hardly a single square foot on the hillside was free of a human missive. The dry Karakoram was nowhere near as forgiving of human abuse as the monsoon-drenched highlands of Nepal might be. Here, human activity was preserved like wood in a petrified forest to greet the eyes of all comers. We looked the other way, we held our noses when the wind blew, and we left.

A day later John and I took off from the group to hike three stages in a day to Askole. We planned to pay a runner to dash out to Dasso to arrange two jeeps for us, thus saving yet another day in the schedule. Just after we passed the toe of the Biafo Glacier, we came upon a lone Englishman, Nick Estcourt, who was a member of the Ogre expedition. Estcourt was trying to arrange air evacuation for Doug Scott and Chris Bonington; they had been injured on Ogre while our party was on Trango.

What a difference luck—or fate—can make in the quality of experience on a mountain. At about the time our party was relaxing in its final bivouac at 19,000 feet on Trango, the British expedition on Ogre, only twenty miles away, was having an entirely different experience. Doug Scott was crawling the last yards into base camp over rough moraine with both legs broken. He and Chris Bonington had reached the summit of the 23,900-foot Ogre on the evening we had reached our base camp. All the while we were waiting out the storm in camp, Scott was descending on his knees, day after day, until he had worn through four layers of clothing and his knees had become numb and swollen.

The ordeal had begun on the first rappel from the summit, where he had slipped on a diagonal traverse and fell a hundred feet into a rock corner. "I've broken me legs!" he yelled to Bonington, who, having feared him dead and for once not choosing words with great care, replied, "Thank God!" As the two descended, Bonington also fell and injured himself. He had several broken ribs, frostbitten fingers, perhaps a broken wrist, and total loss of his voice from laryngitis.

While we were talking with Nick Estcourt, a helicopter flew over our heads. I was shocked, because it was the first aircraft we had seen. Nick was even more shocked, because the helicopter was a day early and neither man was in a position to be picked up.

Estcourt was on his fifth Himalayan expedition with Bonington, and although there had been fatalities on Annapurna and Everest Southwest Face, the Ogre had come the closest to being a full tragedy. Only by incredible tenacity had Scott and Bonington reached the empty base camp—where they read Nick Estcourt's note: "In the unlikely event of your reading this I have gone down for help."

The helicopter returned the following day and plucked Scott from a stretcher just as the rest of our expedition arrived. It was to return in an hour for Bonington, but it didn't come back. We decided that Bonington should wait in Askole for the chopper, while Nick Estcourt and another climber, Clive Rowlands, joined us on the trek out. Our two doctors were able to treat Bonington with their medical kits, but they wanted to follow up in the hospital as soon as possible.

After the great success of our goat-induced fast approach, we hoped to cut at least a day from our schedule going out. We asked our captain to request porters who would carry the normal three days to Dasso in two. "No, that is impossible," he told us, refusing to translate. I located the village's medical officer, who spoke some English, and within minutes Dennis and I were able to hire a full crew of twelve.

Upper left
*Moonlight on
25,660-foot
Masherbrum, from
19,000 feet on
Trango Tower*
Upper right
*John Roskelley,
Galen Rowell,
and Kim Schmitz
on top of
Great Trango Tower.
K2 and Mustagh
Tower rise between
Rowell and Schmitz*
Right
*Panorama from
Urdukas on the
Baltoro Glacier,
where "blocks of
rock, often capped
with ice, rise
vertically for
8,000 feet, for
all the world like
mammoth skyscrapers."*

Forty-eight hours after leaving Askole, we were eating breakfast in a luxurious home in the American community in Islamabad, guests of the Newberg family of U.S.A.I.D. Not only had we made the three-day walk in two, but we had also made some remarkable connections for an evening jeep ride to Skardu and a 4:30 A.M. flight. Poor Chris was not flown out from Askole for another four days, because the chopper needed repairs after a near-crash-landing with Doug.

Our round trip from Islamabad to the summit of Great Trango had taken only twenty-four days, by far the fastest expedition in history to a peak in the Baltoro region. Speed, however, had been incidental to more important goals. We had added a modern twist to Shipton's dream of exploring lower peaks with "a few classic tools and a few friends." Technical rock and ice skills combined with a carefully chosen route had enabled us to follow a single line of weakness up a most difficult-appearing face. We had set no new standards of height or difficulty, but we had certainly experienced a new dimension of pleasure and set an example for the future.

Shipton, when asked to describe his training program for expeditions, once replied, "I have never been guilty of an athletic act!" Today's Himalayan climbers are a new breed trained on the great rock walls of Yosemite and the Alps, toughened by regimens of running, bouldering, and specialized gymnastics. They are part of an age in which travel to the Himalaya has become commonplace. They seek technical challenges, great walls of rock and ice that rise unbroken to the summit. Some of these goals have already been met, not a few by the use of fixed ropes, fixed camps, and great expenditures of time. Alpine-style technical climbing in the Himalaya is in its infancy, and if we proved nothing else we proved that satisfaction is not proportional to altitude or to the number of days spent climbing.

This simple realization is nothing new. Shipton had it long before Nepal was opened to expeditions. He foresaw a time when advances in technique and equipment would open up a boundless horizon of fresh mountain endeavors, but he always considered the human element before the needs of the enterprise.

"The strongest mountaineering party," he wrote, "is one in which each member has implicit confidence in all his companions, recognizes their vital importance to the common effort and feels himself to have an indispensable part to play . . . To my mind it can only be achieved with a relatively small, closely-knit party . . . Remove, then, the impression that one is engaged in a vast enterprise upon which the eyes of the world are focused, realize that one is setting out to climb a mountain . . . and one will add greatly to one's chances of success, and, more important still, enjoyment."

True to Shipton's dream, my fondest memories are not of the summit or the surmounting of difficulties on the ascent. After the climb I sat on a boulder near base camp with my bare feet dangled into a cluster of wildflowers, the same boulder on which I had sat looking for the snow leopard just four days earlier. The world seemed to flow with new simplicity and clarity. I lost my sense of time and I have no idea how long I was there. A cloud passed in front of the sun, and I shivered as a breeze off the glacier hit my bare skin. Before walking back to camp I wrote in my journal, "I have found Shangri-La but no one can travel there, for it is not a place, but a state of mind."

Stormy sunset at
Trango basecamp, Pakistan

Left
Uli Biaho Tower,
Karakoram Himalaya

Above
John Roskelley and
Uli Biaho Tower
from 17,500 on
Great Trango Tower

Epilogue

Several members of the three 1977 expeditions in this book returned to the Himalaya in 1978 and 1979. John Roskelley took part in four expeditions that resulted in three major successes. After his lone failure, an alpine-style attempt on the north face of Jannu (25,294 feet) with Kim Schmitz, he reached the summit of K2 without oxygen (28,250 feet) as a member of Jim Whittaker's second K2 expedition in the summer of 1978. The following spring, accompanied by one Sherpa, he made the first ascent of Gaurishankar—a coveted, extremely difficult summit on the Tibet-Nepal border which was long thought to be the highest mountain in the world because of its isolated position, although it is actually just 23,440 feet. With him on the expedition were Schmitz, Dennis Hennek, and Jim Morrissey. In the summer of 1979, Roskelley led an alpine-style climb of the east face of Uli Biaho Tower in the Karakoram just across the valley from the Trango Towers. Schmitz was also a member of this four-man team, which accomplished what may well be the most difficult technical climb yet done in the Himalaya. Thus John Roskelley has firmly established himself as this generation's most accomplished American mountaineer in the Himalaya.

In 1978 Dr. Gordon Benner of the Nun Kun Expedition led a Sierra Club party around Annapurna and partway up Thorungtse. Maynard Cohick reached the top of Peak Communism (24,548 feet) in the Soviet Pamirs in 1978 and joined fellow Nun Kun summitters Peter Cummings and Pat O'Donnell on a semialpine-style expedition to Annapurna in 1979. An avalanche wiped out the high camp, killing Cohick only forty minutes after O'Donnell and Cummings had left for the next camp. After the tragedy, heavy snow continued to fall on the upper mountain, and the climb was abandoned.

Three of the members of the British Ogre Expedition that we met in the Karakoram attempted the unclimbed West Ridge of K2 in 1978 with a moderate-sized expedition led by Chris Bonington. Nick Estcourt was swept away in an avalanche while roped to Doug Scott, who was snatched from certain death a second time in less than a year when the fixed line connecting him to Estcourt broke, leaving him standing alone on the empty snows of K2. In 1979 Scott again went to the Himalaya with a small party that climbed Kanchenjunga (28,146 feet) in alpine style without oxygen.

Since 1977 I have returned to the Himalaya twice. Jo Sanders and I spent the Christmas of 1978 in Nepal, seeing old friends, researching this book, and trekking in the Khumbu region. Kim Schmitz and I, together with adventure-skier Ned Gillette, succeeded on a grand traverse of the Karakoram Range late in the winter of 1979-80. No peaks were climbed as Nordic skis were used to carry 120-pound loads as high as 22,500 feet without porters along a 285-mile route following the Himalaya's largest glaciers—the Siachen, Baltoro, Biafo, and Hispar—which nearly interconnect like a string of lakes.

As this book goes to press in mid-1980, I'm heading for another part of the Himalaya as yet untouched by modern tourism. Jo, Ned Gillette, and I comprise half of a small expedition of friends bound for Mustagh Ata, "The Father of Ice Mountains." The stated goal of this first American mountaineering expedition to China is to climb the 24,757-foot peak without porters and ski from the top. As always, however, the unintentional delight of discovery of a new country, its people, and its high wilderness are more of a lure than the summit.

A Note on the Photography

Both mountaineering and photography in the Himalaya have undergone modern revolutions that pose similar dilemmas. The early goals were narrow and well defined: to reach a high summit by any means and to produce a high-quality collection of images. Success in both fields was limited by constraints the participants imposed upon themselves. Pioneer photographers moved through the Himalaya with great burdens of equipment, and I hesitate to provide a list of my own before making it clear that equipment choices are far down the line of variables that make for good photography. The eye, not the camera, produces the sharp, uncluttered vision behind every great photograph.

The greatest of the early lensmen, Vittorio Sella, is famed for landscapes that approach technical and artistic perfection. There is a uniform stillness about them that critics impart to Sella's chosen style, but practically speaking it is no more than the inability of his cumbersome equipment to document fleeting moments. A Sherpa's spontaneous smile or the distant motion of wild sheep were beyond his reach.

Photography now can come closer to the movement and soul of Himalayan experience. The path is as yet unsigned, and choices are made by intuition rather than instruction. With today's camera, any amateur can bring back a few prize images; the challenge is to produce a meaningful whole. My goal has been to present as wide a range of objective and artistic reality as possible without obvious gimmicks. Modern 35 mm equipment allows me to produce landscapes on fine-grained Kodachrome that will stand up to poster-sized enlargements, and also to record the all-important moments of human existence. The 35-mm medium is surprisingly unforgiving, however. Only Kodachrome transparency films give me adequate sharpness and color, but they allow so little latitude in exposure that many lighting conditions are simply impossible to render. There is always the temptation to hand-hold scenics and close-ups along the trail, but only by using a 35-mm camera in the mode of a larger format camera—on a tripod with great depth of field and careful composition—can the results be visually similar.

Film is the cheapest item of a Himalayan photo jaunt. I have yet to hear of a photographer who thought he carried too much. Many have brought too little, and have had dreadful experiences with color film purchased in Asia. I have suffered in this regard from both heat- and age-damaged film. One batch purchased at a major camera store in Kathmandu proved to be exposed film of someone else's trip to India, apparently stolen, rewound, and sealed into Kodak boxes.

The equipment I don't use is more revealing of my style than that which I bring along. No zooms, fish-eyes, or strong filters. Zooms are too slow for color work, both in handling and in light-gathering power, optical considerations notwithstanding. My widest lens is a 20-mm, which gives no distortions that are not already inherent in human vision. My strongest filter is a Nikon A2, which adds a salmon tinge to cut the bluish cast from shadows under a clear sky. I use polarizers about 10 percent of the time to cut haze or intensify colors that have been dulled by refraction from the blue sky. I rarely use one on the snow, where already dark skies tend to go black and colors are purified naturally by the sun's reflection from a white surface.

For going light on a climb or day trip, I carry a Nikon FM with 24 mm and 105 mm lenses. On the trail or on an expedition with porters, I bring along an extra camera and 20-mm, 35-mm, 55-mm, 200-mm, and 500-mm lenses plus a sturdy Star-D tripod. This range of equipment allows me to preserve the reality of a scene while intensifying it by saturating colors, simplifying lines, and cropping out extraneous material. I find photographing the Himalaya as difficult as climbing its summits.

Index

Selected index of people and places
(Page numbers in bold refer to photo captions.)

Display type was hand set
in Belwe Medium and Light.

Text was set in Palatino by Graphics
West/Typeline, Seattle.

Color separations, printing and binding
by Dai Nippon Printing Co., Ltd.,
Tokyo.